Love Begins At Fifty

Raymond Hopkins

www.silvermonpublishing.co.uk

© 1998 Raymond Hopkins

PUBLISHING

A Division of Silvermoon Productions Limited
3rd Floor I 207 Regent Street I London I W1B 3HH
0207 096 0979
www.silvermoonpublishing.co.uk

ISBN 978-1-910457-09-2

Silvermoon Publishing is an innovative publishing house established to publish plays and license rights to theatre companies world-wide. Silvermoon aims to promote its plays and playwrights to ensure that its playwrights get maximum exposure.

Rights of performance for Silvermoon plays are controlled by Silvermoon Publishing, 3rd Floor, 207 Regent Street, London W1B 3HH who will issue a performing licence on payment of a fee and subject to a number of conditions. These plays are fully protected under the Copyright Laws of the British Commonwealth of Nations, the United States of America and all countries of the Berne and Universal Copyright Conventions. All rights, including stage, motion picture, radio, television, public reading and translation into foreign languages are strictly reserved. It is an infringement of the copyright to give any performance or public reading of these plays before the fee has been paid and the licence issued. The royalty fee is subject to contract and subject to variation at the sole discretion of Silvermoon Publishing. In territories overseas the fees quoted in this catalogue may not apply. A fee will be quoted on application to Silvermoon Publishing.

The right of Raymond Hopkins to be identified as author of this work has been asserted by him in accordance with Section 77 of the Copyright, Designs and Patents Act 1988

COPYRIGHT INFORMATION

No part of this publication may lawfully be reproduced in ANY form or by any means - photocopying, typescript, recording (including video-recording), manuscript, electronic, mechanical or otherwise - or be transmitted or stored in a retrieval system, without prior permission.

Licenses for amateur performances are issued subject to the understanding that it shall be made clear in all advertising matter that the audience will witness an amateur performance; that the names of the authors of the plays shall be included on all programmes, and that the integrity of the authors' work will be preserved.

The Royalty Fee is subject to contract and subject to variation at the sole discretion of Silvermoon Publishing.

In Theatres of Halls seating Four Hundred or more the fee will be subject to negotiation.

In Territories Overseas the fee quoted may not apply. A fee will be quoted on application to Silvermoon Publishing, London.

Recordings of the songs mentioned in the text are not covered by licences issued by Silvermoon Publishing. The use of these recordings should be declared to the PERFORMING RIGHTS SOCIETY in the usual manner.

VIDEO-RECORDING OF AMATEUR PRODUCTIONS

Please note that the copyright laws governing video-recording are extremely complex and that it should not be assumed that any play may be video-recorded for whatever purpose without first obtaining the permission of the appropriate agents. The fact that a play is published by Silvermoon Publishing does not indicate that video rights are available or that Silvermoon Publishing control such rights.

PERFORMING LICENCE APPLICATIONS

A performing licence for these plays will be issued by "Silvermoon Publishing" subject to the following conditions:-

1. That the performance fee is paid in full on the date of application for a licence.
2. That the name of the author(s) is/are clearly shown in any programme or publicity material.
3. That the author(s) is/are entitled to receive two complimentary tickets to see his/her/their work in performance if they so wish.
4. That a copy of the play is purchased from Silvermoon Publishing for each named speaking part and a minimum of three copies purchased for backstage use.
5. That a copy of any reviews / Marketing materials be forwarded to Silvermoon Publishing.
6. That the Silvermoon Publishing licensing statement be displayed on any marketing material.

FEES

Details of script prices and fees payable for each performance or public reading can be obtained by telephone to (+44) 0207 0961603 or to the address below. Alternatively, latest prices can be obtained from our website. www.silvermoonpublishing.co.uk.

To apply for a performing licence for any play please write to Silvermoon Publishing, 3rd Floor, 207 Regent Street, London W1B 3HH or email via our website with the following details:-

1. Name and address of theatre company.
2. Details of venue including seating capacity.
3. Dates of proposed performance or public reading.
4. Contact telephone number for Author's complimentary tickets.

Or apply directly via our website at www.silvermoonpublishing.co.uk

PROFESSIONAL RIGHTS

Professional rights for Nativity should be addressed to Silvermoon Publishing.

The author of LOVE BEGINS AT FIFTY, Raymond Hopkins, is donating his share of the proceeds to MULTIPLE SCLEROSIS RESEARCH.

CAST IN ORDER OF APPEARANCE

ANITA DEBANKS
About fifty-two. Well educated. Feels that she has married beneath herself, and consequently, treats her husband with contempt. She has immaculate dress sense.

CLIVE DEBANKS
About forty-nine. A romantic who has been starved of love and affection by his wife. Happy to let the world go by. Very easy going. Not much dress sense.

JACK REYNOLDS
About forty-eight. Confirmed bachelor, who likes female company, without any commitment. Down to earth and lives for today. Full of charisma. A lifelong friend of Clive Debanks.

CLAIRE MURPHY
About fifty-three. Slightly overweight, with a poor dress sense. Has habit of misinterpreting a situation and will often say the wrong thing. A lifelong friend of Anita Debanks.

TRACY BARTON (*Daughter of Clive and Anita*)
About twenty-three. Has lots of her mother's traits, although she does have a compassionate side to her nature. Likes keeping up with modern fashion and makes the best of her appearance. Lives on an emotional roller coaster.

ANNABEL WICKSON
About twenty-seven. Slim, and very good looking. Can be outspoken. Searching for a fun life, after being torn apart by the break-up of her parents' marriage.

MAVIS LEGGETT
About sixty-five. Gives the appearance of being slightly doddery but is always able to hold her own. She dresses in quirky clothes. An eccentric.

EMILY ROBERTS
About forty-two. Very attractive with a good figure. Comes from a poor background. Has never married. Kind and considerate. Painfully shy.

HENRY CLARKE
About forty. A Cockney with a lot of silly chatter. Has a happy-go-lucky attitude to life. A flash dresser.

SUZIE - The goldfish.

LOVE BEGINS AT FIFTY

ACT ONE
Scene I - Wednesday late morning.
(*Six weeks before the fiftieth birthday party*)
Scene II - The following Tuesday evening.
Scene III - Friday afternoon. (*Three weeks later*)

ACT TWO
Scene I - Friday morning. (*Two weeks later*)
Scene II - Saturday afternoon. (*The fiftieth birthday party*)

The Debanks live in a large town in the South of England.

The action of the play takes place in the lounge of their semi-detached house. It is late spring.

LOVE BEGINS AT FIFTY was first presented on 25th June 1998, by the Hanborough Players with the following cast:–

        Anita Debanks .... Denise Ball
        Clive Debanks .... Nigel James
        Jack Reynolds .... Chas Simpkins
        Claire Murphy .... Heather Nisbet
        Tracy Barton .... Nicola Ball
        Annabel Wickson .... Emily James
        Mavis Leggett .... Elizabeth Margetts
        Emily Roberts .... Louise Brown
        Henry Clarke .... Andrew Hester
        Suzie .... Guest appearance

The play was directed by JACKY HOPKINS

ACT I
Scene I

As the curtain rises Anita is sitting on the sofa reading the minutes of a committee meeting. Clive enters from the hall carrying an old record player and some forty-five R.P.M. records.

ANITA Did you put those books in the loft for me?

CLIVE Yes, and you'll never guess what I've just discovered up there.

(*Standing record player on floor*)

ANITA (*Engrossed in reading minutes*) All the tools you can never find when a job needs doing around the house?

CLIVE No, I've only just found the first record player I ever owned, and some of my original forty-fives.

ANITA (*Looking at record player*) That's a bit of luck. (*Pause*) The dustmen are calling tomorrow.

CLIVE Are you joking? This is part of my history.

ANITA (*Sarcastically*) So what are you going to do? Preserve it for posterity, along with your glowing school reports?

CLIVE I'll have you know this is a Dansette player, with full auto changer. I was the envy of the street when I bought this.

ANITA (*Totally uninterested*) If you say so.

CLIVE I drove my mum crazy when I harmonised along with Gerry and the Pacemakers. (*Singing*) How do you do what you do to me, I wish I knew, if I …? (*Clive puts record player on the table*)

ANITA Yes I'm sure you did. You're not putting that thing on my polished table, are you?

CLIVE I want to see if it still works.

ANITA That table's already covered in burns, after your efforts to repair the toaster finished up with an explosion.

CLIVE (*Aside*) Pity you didn't blow up with it.

(*Clive mutters under his breath. He starts to look inside the record player and clean it. The phone rings. Anita answers it*)

ANITA Hello … Yes … Just a moment. (*Anita looks through her diary*) The only night I'm free next week is Thursday … Right, I'll pencil you in … Bye. (*Replaces receiver*) I've got every night out next week.

CLIVE (*Still fiddling with record player*) You've only got yourself to blame, dear, considering you're involved with every organisation from "Transvestites have the right to wear tights" to "Frogs need freedom to frolic."

ANITA It's a pity more people aren't aware of their social responsibilities.

CLIVE I hardly ever see you now, and when you are here, you're either phoning one of your committee members or making fairy cakes for the mayor's funny friends.

ANITA Oh that reminds me, the mayor's going to say a few words at your fiftieth birthday party.

CLIVE He'll have a job. He's not even been invited.

ANITA Yes he has. I asked him yesterday, and he said he'd be only too pleased to come along.

CLIVE Well thanks for telling me. (Pause) It's funny that when I suggested asking Bert and his missus, you said there wouldn't be room.

ANITA We're certainly not having that woman. She used to be a stripper.

CLIVE Well, we've all got to make a living.

ANITA I agree. But, after a couple of gins, she thinks she's back on stage and starts shedding all her clothes. And I really don't think the vicar's blood pressure's up to that.

CLIVE If it was up to me, I wouldn't have a party. I mean, what is there to celebrate?

ANITA The fact that you've reached the ripe old age of fifty.

CLIVE Exactly. So all the under fifties'll be gloating at me and all the over fifties'll be telling me which parts of my body'll be dropping off next. By the end of the party, I'll probably be suicidal.

ANITA By the way, did I tell you I'm attending a W.I. conference in Birmingham next Tuesday? I'll be staying overnight and back Wednesday afternoon.

CLIVE And what's on the agenda this time? (*Sarcastically*) The plight of the pot-bellied pig?

ANITA Actually I've been asked to represent our local branch at the A.G.M. It's a great honour.

CLIVE You spend more time in committee meetings than the chairman of ICI.

ANITA You mean chairperson. We have to be politically correct nowadays.

CLIVE What a load of rubbish, or should I say recyclable refuse? (*Putting his arm around Anita*) Let's spend this afternoon together, reliving the sounds of the sixties.

ANITA (*Pulling Clive's arm away*) No thank you, the sixties did nothing for me.

CLIVE Did you ever try the Horace Batchelor infra-draw method?

ANITA Don't be so crude. Trust you to bring sex up at every opportunity.

CLIVE It had nothing to do with sex. He was on Radio Luxembourg. Horace Batchelor told you how to win the football pools. Keynsham, spelt K.E.Y.N.S …

ANITA I don't know what you're on about.

CLIVE What about Hughie Green on the telly? "I mean that most sincerely folks, I really do." And the day we won the World Cup?

ANITA	(*Sarcastically*) If you'd have told me we were going to be waltzing down memory lane, I'd have put my ball gown on.
CLIVE	They were the best years of my life, young, single and carefree. That is until I met you.
ANITA	Really? So where does our twenty-eight years of marriage fit into your ratings?
CLIVE	(*Aside*) I'd need to seek legal advice before answering that.
ANITA	I'm popping over to the printers to collect your birthday invitations. (*Angrily*) We'll continue this conversation when I get back.

(*Anita exits to hall. Clive plugs in record player and puts on a record of The Swinging Blue Jeans singing "Hippy Hippy Shake"*)

CLIVE	(*With elation*) It works. That's fantastic. (*Clive makes out he's playing a guitar. He jumps around the room. The doorbell rings. Clive exits to hall holding his back - off*) Hello, Jack, come in. (*Clive and Jack enter*)
JACK	They don't make records like this anymore. (*Walking over to the record player*) That's a Dansette player isn't it?
CLIVE	Yea, and it worked after all these years.
JACK	The first time I ever heard this record was at a Youth Club dance. I spent all night plucking up enough courage to ask this gorgeous girl if she'd do the twist with me.
CLIVE	So what did she say? (*Turning record off*)
JACK	"Drop dead!"
CLIVE	Do you realise they were the best years of our lives? Everything was new and exciting.
JACK	We certainly had some laughs.
CLIVE	What do you remember most about your teenage years?

JACK	Mods and Rockers, The Beatles, espresso coffee, the mini.
CLIVE	What car or skirt?
JACK	I remember them both, with great affection.
CLIVE	Everything was priced in guineas. And you always got double Green Shield stamps on Fridays.
JACK	(*Reflectively*) My first motor bike, a Triumph Tiger Cub. That was a real little mover.
CLIVE	So was your first girl friend. She certainly hadn't got any inhibitions.
JACK	(*With affection*) Oh yes, dear Carol Jones. I passed her onto you, when she'd finished awakening me to the pleasures of the flesh.
CLIVE	I was a late developer, (pause) well that is until I met Carol.
JACK	You could always spot the boy she was dating. He'd have a dazed look about him, with a satisfied smile on his face.
CLIVE	(*Looking thoughtful*) She gave me my first kiss. (*With feeling*) It was one of the most mind-blowing experiences of my whole life.
JACK	They used to say it was the eighth wonder of the world. How she fitted that long tongue of hers back into her mouth. In fact she got nicknamed "Lizard Lips."
CLIVE	(*Smiling*) It's all coming back to me. She'd had a few drinks, and a pay rise at work, so I knew I was onto a winner. By the end of the night, I'd graduated from nursery school to university, and I finished up with a first class honours degree in Carnal Knowledge. I want to do it all again. (*Looking thoughtful*) No, I do. (*Getting excited*) I WANT TO DO IT ALL AGAIN!!
JACK	What are you on about?

CLIVE   I want to find another Carol Jones, and relive all those magical moments. I want to re-awaken all those incredible passionate feelings, those sensual experiences, that I'd almost forgotten about.

JACK   Don't be stupid, that's all history now. You'll soon be a fully fledged wrinkly.

CLIVE   Hang on a minute. I'm not even fifty yet.

JACK   You will be in six weeks. Look, if you're getting a bit frisky, best to have a word with your wife.

CLIVE   Are you joking? (*Holding goldfish bowl in the air*) You've got a higher sex drive than my wife, haven't you, Suzie? (*Putting goldfish bowl back on cupboard*)

JACK   I've never seen a goldfish making love.

CLIVE   Exactly. (*Looking thoughtful*) My wife should be charged with murder, because, over the years, she's killed off all my emotional passion.

JACK   There must have been some feelings when you first got married.

CLIVE   Whatever feelings we had, have gone. We've drifted apart. We only talk when we're arguing. There's no warmth or affection between us. The only thing we've got in common is the joint mortgage.

JACK   In other words, you're just a typical married couple.

CLIVE   I'm finding a girl who's looking for romance and affection. Then, together we'll recapture all those wonderful feelings, which'll get the blood pumping round my body till I …

JACK   Have a heart attack. (*Pause*) Look, if you want some excitement, join the Old Folks Club.

CLIVE   (*Getting excited*) Can you remember when it was all new? Your hormones had just kicked in, and your hands were going walkabouts, discovering the uncharted territory of the female body?

JACK		So what's awakened all these dormant, passionate feelings?
CLIVE		Finding my old record player, listening to the sounds of my youth. It's given me a yearning for one last taste of life before they nail me in my box.
JACK		And what's your wife going to say about this extra-marital activity?
CLIVE		Well actually, I wasn't going to tell her.
JACK		But she's given you twenty-eight years of her life.
CLIVE		No, she's stolen twenty-eight years of mine.
JACK		So what about the sanctity of marriage?
CLIVE		In front of two hundred people my wife said that she'd love, honour and obey me. She was lying.
JACK		And I suppose you've been a good boy.
CLIVE		I've never been unfaithful. I've led a blameless married life, and I've put up with my wife's constant nagging. (*Depressingly*) There's got to be more to life than this. I've forgotten what it's like to have fun.
JACK		When you're married, that's as good as it gets. You should have stayed single like me. No woman'll ever tie me down.
CLIVE		I've made up my mind. There's a girl out there, just waiting for me to light her flame of desire.
JACK		You're really intent on this madness, aren't you?
CLIVE		Too true, and I've got fifty quid that says I'll do it.
JACK		Why don't we make it a hundred? You never were much of a super stud.
CLIVE		Give me two weeks. I'll have found a girl, relived my dreams, and taken your hundred quid.

JACK Before you get the money, I'll want positive proof you've scored.

CLIVE So what are you suggesting – I nick her bra?

JACK (*Looking thoughtful*) No, you want to be a teenager again, come back with a love-bite.

CLIVE You're on. (*Clive and Jack shake hands*) This'll be the easiest money I've ever made. You're always seeing the rich and famous with a pretty girl on their arm.

JACK But you're not rich or famous. Your face has got more wrinkles than corrugated cardboard. The only wave you've got left in your hair is the one that's waving goodbye, and you look six months pregnant. So what have you got to offer?

CLIVE (*Thinking*) Experience!!

JACK Even if you do find a wrinkly who's interested, she'll be too worn out to do anything. Her false teeth'll probably drop out when she's giving you the love bite.

CLIVE It sounds as though you're getting worried already.

JACK And where are you going to find this "wonder woman?"

CLIVE (*Picking up newspaper and looking through it*) Lonely hearts adverts. There's everything here from Father Christmas wants a fairy to Big Ben needs someone with time on their hands.

JACK I'll tell you something, you'll never find a woman with all the qualities you desire.

CLIVE You could be right. (*Looking thoughtful*) Best to be on the safe side. I'll get three round here, and then make a final choice.

JACK So you think they'll all just stand around while you're making up your mind?

CLIVE My wife's away next Tuesday night. I'll invite the girls round at one hour intervals, assess their potential, then

	select one for the second date, (*looking pleased with himself*) and that's when we'll make sweet music together.
JACK	You always were tone deaf. (*Pause*) So what age group are you looking for?
CLIVE	As young as possible. I might as well go out with a bang.
JACK	I suppose it would help if they can remember their teenage years.
CLIVE	(*Reading the paper*) Could you loan me a pen, please? I want to mark some prospective partners.
JACK	(*Handing over pen*) You be careful, that could be incriminating evidence.
CLIVE	(*Circling advert*) Here's one "Forty-two-year-old woman, who's forgotten what the word fun means. Looking for a man with a dictionary, so we can discover the meaning of true happiness together."

(*Suggestion - You could split the word dictionary by saying ¬dic- then pausing to turn the newspaper page, after which you complete the word -tionary*)

JACK	You don't know what she looks like, she's probably a real old dragon.
CLIVE	Here's another "Birthday girl, is looking for a man who's hot enough to light all the candles on her cake."
JACK	That woman's dangerous, she'll kill you.
CLIVE	Yea, but what a way to go. (*Clive circles advert*) That's two sorted out, one left. (*Looking through adverts*) I've not had so much fun in years. Ah, here we are, "I've just found the secret of life, why don't you let me show it to you?" (*Clive circles the advert*) That's it, I've got three. Hang on a minute I must have this one. "Good looking nymphomaniac, with slender firm body, seeks mature man with experience to help with her thesis on the Kamasutra."

JACK	(*Trying to grab paper*) Give me that paper, I'll ring her.
CLIVE	(*Pulling paper away*) Only kidding. (*They both start to laugh. Anita and Claire enter from hall*)
ANITA	What are you two laughing at?
CLIVE	(*Looking guilty*) Oh nothing, we were just …um…
JACK	(*Unconvincingly*) Doing the crossword. (*Clive puts paper under sofa cushion*)
ANITA	I bumped into Claire at the printers, and we've decided to go shopping.
CLAIRE	I've got to book a perm at the hairdressers.
JACK	(*Sarcastically - aside*) That'll be a total waste of money.
CLAIRE	(*Getting cross*) What do you mean, a waste of money?
JACK	(*Looking embarrassed*) Um … Well … You can't improve on what's already perfect.
CLAIRE	Oh Jack, you dear man, how kind of you.
JACK	(*Breathing a sigh of relief*) It's time I went, I only popped in to see if you fancied a drink tonight. They've got a Karaoke competition, at the Nag's Head.
CLIVE	I'm game for a bit of that. (*Looking at Anita*) Fancy coming along, dear? We could give them a bit of Sonny and Cher.
ANITA	Don't be ridiculous, I've got far more important things to do with my time.
JACK	(*To Clive*) I'll see you down there about eight then. We could double up as the Everly Brothers.
ANITA	I'm sure the landlord'll love that. (*Sarcastically*) He could put you on at closing time, when he wants to empty his pub.

CLIVE	Come and have a look at my roses, Jack, they're the best I've ever grown. (*Exits to kitchen with Jack*)
ANITA	I'll just pop and get a shopping bag. (*Anita exits to hall. Claire sits on the sofa and discovers the newspaper. She starts to read it. Anita enters from hall with shopping bag*)
CLAIRE	Look what I've just found in the paper. (*Reading from paper*) "How would you like a free Caribbean cruise?"
ANITA	I'd love one please, what's the catch?
CLAIRE	"A competition sponsored by the local paper to promote the importance of marriage. We are looking for couples who've been married over twenty-five years."
ANITA	(*Sounding depressed*) We've been married twenty-eight.
CLAIRE	They're offering the winning couple the chance of a second honeymoon …
ANITA	There's the catch, a second honeymoon. The ghastly nightmares of my first one still haunt me.
CLAIRE	Don't be stupid, you won't have to … well, you know. (*Reading from the paper*) "Enjoy six weeks of fun and relaxation, whilst travelling around the Caribbean on a luxury liner."
ANITA	This sounds too good to be true. How do I enter?
CLAIRE	(*Reading from the newspaper*) "One simple phone call, giving details of your family life and revealing the secret of your marital success."
ANITA	A cocktail of tranquillisers, washed down with gallons of alcohol, have played an important role. (*Pause*) Actually, I'm going for it. I've got nothing to lose. What's the number?
CLAIRE	736841

ANITA (*Dialling number*) Well, I mean surely I deserve some reward for all the years of misery and sacrifice I've endured. (*Speaking into phone*) Hello … I wish to enter your competition for the perfect married couple … Twenty-eight years of sheer bliss … Never a cross word. (*Anita holds her crossed fingers in the air*) We do everything together … Hobbies, yes I'm always very busy with lots of charity work … Oh, right … Mrs. Anita Debanks, 56 Malom Way - phone number 747423 … Right, so you'll ring first … Oh, what a coincidence, that's the same day as my darling husband's fiftieth birthday … Thank you… Bye. (*Replaces receiver*)

CLAIRE Well, what did they say?

ANITA I've got to send a letter saying how ecstatically happy we've been during our twenty-eight years of marriage. You don't think I could get prosecuted for making false statements do you?

CLAIRE Not so long as your husband backs up your story.

ANITA I'm not telling that mindless moron about the competition. Once he opens his mouth, we don't stand a chance.

CLAIRE He'll have to know at some point, after all he is the other half of this marriage made in heaven.

ANITA I suppose you're right, but I'll keep him in the dark as long as possible. The trouble is they're sending a photographer to get pictures of the happy couple.

CLAIRE I suppose you could lie, and say it's part of a secret birthday surprise.

ANITA Oh, that reminds me, the results are being announced the same day as his fiftieth birthday.

CLAIRE If you won, you'd really have something to celebrate. (*Pause*) I'd have a word with the mayor. It doesn't hurt to do a bit of name dropping on things like this.

ANITA You're right, I'll give him a ring a bit later.

CLAIRE	I'd say you were in with a real chance. You've got the winning combination – two happily married children, you're a pillar of society and your husband's …
ANITA	Well, we can't expect everything to be perfect. (*Tracy enters from hall carrying a suitcase*) Hello, darling. I didn't realize you were going on holiday.
TRACY	Oh, Mum, my whole world's falling apart, I hate that swine, I wish I'd never married him. (*Tracy bursts into tears*) I'm moving back home with you.
CLAIRE	What's he done, Tracy? Why have you left him?
TRACY	He's packing up his job in the city, and getting out of the rat race. He's selling our semi, buying a bus (*pause*) and becoming a hippie. (*Tracy is now in floods of tears*) He says we're all getting too materialistic, and he's going back to basics. (*Pause*) I need a drink, Mummy. You didn't tell me that marriage was going to be like this. (*Tracy pours out a drink*)
CLAIRE	What's got into the boy? I always had him down as a sensible lad.
ANITA	Men are like dogs, they've got to be trained to do what they're told.
TRACY	(*Stops crying*) I'm not living in a bus, there won't be room for my dishwasher or tumble drier. (*Looking horrified*) What about my bidet? (*Tracy takes a long drink*)
CLAIRE	(*To Anita*) This isn't going to look very good on your competition entry form.
TRACY	I've just had a horrible thought, it's not free love in these communes, is it?
CLAIRE	I think they share everything, including wives. It's all part of their culture.
TRACY	I won't be able to keep going. I'll have to tell them I've got a permanent headache!

CLAIRE　　Don't worry. (*Pause*) They'll have you on drugs within a week, so you won't be aware of what's happening.

TRACY　　I need to talk to Dad, and get things sorted out.

ANITA　　It's no good talking to him. Get your case. (*Forcefully*) We'll go and have a word with this husband of yours. I'll soon make him face up to his responsibilities.

TRACY　　Thank you, Mum. I don't want to spend my days milking goats or eating my Sunday roast in the top of a tree to stop a new bypass being built. Please make him see sense.

ANITA　　When I've finished with him, he'll have a job to see anything. Let's go.

(*Tracy picks up her case. Anita, Claire and Tracy exit to hall. Clive enters from kitchen. He picks up the newspaper, reads it, then picks up phone, and dials a number*)

CLIVE　　Hello, I'm replying to your advert in the personal column … I'd love to meet you. Would it be possible to see you next Tuesday? My address is 56 Malom Way. A good time to call would be …

Scene II

As the curtain rises, Clive is sitting on the sofa. (*Suggestion - He has one sock off and he is clipping his toe-nails, with a large pair of scissors, into a waste paper bin*) *He lights the two candles which are stood on the table. The doorbell rings. He quickly covers up the goldfish with a cloth.*

CLIVE　　Sorry, Suzie, but it's best if you don't see anything.
(*He puts on a record of Adam Faith singing "Poor me." He looks around the room. The doorbell rings again. He exits to hall - off*) Oh, it's you Jack, come in. (*Clive and Jack enter. Clive turns record player off*) I thought you were my first date arrived early.

JACK　　(*Looking around the room*) It all looks very nice. I thought I'd better call round and wish you good luck. (*Jack shakes hands with Clive*)

CLIVE　　I haven't been so nervous since I took my driving test.

JACK	The outcome'll probably be the same: failure, due to poor handling ability.
CLIVE	The adrenaline's already pumping. All the hairs on the back of my neck are standing up.
JACK	At your age, it's a miracle that anything's standing up. (*Pause*) I just can't believe you've persuaded all three of them to call round.
CLIVE	It was hard going at first, until I remembered some of my old chat up lines.
JACK	Which one did you use? "Come to my house, and we'll watch Dixon of Dock Green." (*Pause*) So what arrangements have you made? Are they arriving in alphabetical order?
CLIVE	I've given myself an hour with each of them. Then a ten minute gap to recover, jot down their score on the Richter scale, and prepare for the next one.
JACK	In other words, while your coffee's coming to the boil, you'll be assessing whether you can bring them to the boil.
CLIVE	I'm serving a light supper, they'll be choosing from an à la carte menu.
JACK	I didn't realise you had any culinary skills.
CLIVE	I can't even boil an egg, so I've bought some microwave meals from the local supermarket.
JACK	I'm very impressed with your organisation.
CLIVE	(*Looking smug*) I've thought of everything. Here's a list of the evening's events. (*Clive hands a piece of paper to Jack, who reads it carefully*)
JACK	I only hope you're a quick worker. You haven't got them booked in at one hour ten minute gaps. They're arriving every ten minutes.

CLIVE		(*Snatching list from Jack and reading it*) Good grief. I don't believe it.
JACK		What a fiasco.
CLIVE		(*Clive drops to the sofa*) I was panicking when they phoned.
JACK		You'll certainly be panicking when they're all stood here, comparing notes.
CLIVE		For years I've been a one woman man, and now I've got them arriving by the bus load.
JACK		Shall I tell you what's worse than an angry woman? (*Pause*) Three angry women!
CLIVE		Whatever am I going to do?
JACK		Abort the mission and head for the pub.
CLIVE		But I've got a hundred quid bet riding on the evening.
JACK		If you start paying for my drinks tonight, it'll only take you a few weeks to clear your debt.
CLIVE		I'll never get another opportunity like this. I'm not giving up that easily. It just means I've got to get a move on.
JACK		Even Flash Gordon couldn't sort out a prospective partner that quick.
CLIVE		(*Looking thoughtful*) Hang on a minute, I've got it, synchronise watches. What time do you make it? (*Jack and Clive look at their watches*)
JACK		Five to eight.
CLIVE		Spot on, so in five minutes my first date arrives.
JACK		Correct, and ten minutes later, ding dong the doorbell rings and another lustful lady awaits your pleasure.
CLIVE		Your wife's having a baby.

JACK	Now that could be difficult seeing as I'm not married.
CLIVE	Just listen, after each of my dates has been here five minutes, you'll phone to say your wife's having a baby.
JACK	So how will my wife's imminent childbirth solve your over subscribed love nest?
CLIVE	I'm on a mission of mercy. I've got to drive your wife to the hospital immediately.
JACK	So you apologise to your prospective partner, she leaves and you're ready for the next one, brilliant. (*Pause*) It'll never work.
CLIVE	Of course it will. After all, I'm only assessing their potential tonight.
JACK	Well if you're crazy enough to carry on with these auditions, I suppose the least I can do is help you hang yourself.
CLIVE	Don't forget to ring exactly on time. The first call's due at five past eight.
JACK	(*Walking to hall exit*) If any of these grannies lose their bus pass, don't expect me to run them home.
CLIVE	(*Looking sheepish*) Actually I've changed my mind on one of the girls. I've gone for a twenty-seven year old.
JACK	(Walking back into room) Are you completely mad? You haven't got a hope in hell of pulling a twenty-seven year old bird. (*Getting cross*) First you cock up the appointment times, and then you try and score with a girl half your age. With a short-sighted wrinkly you'd have been in with a chance. Especially if you'd smashed her glasses, but not a twenty-seven year old.
CLIVE	(*Looking worried*) I suppose I should have given it a bit more thought. I seem to have got myself into a bit of a predicament.
JACK	I may just be able to save the situation. (*Looking at his watch*) We've just got time. (*Jack runs through

	hall exit. After a few seconds he returns with a carrier bag) I went to a fancy dress party last week as Roy Orbison (Jack hands over wig and sunglasses) Try this on, it's your only hope.
CLIVE	You're not seriously expecting me to wear this are you?
JACK	Who do you think has had the most girl friends - you or Roy Orbison? If it works for him it'll work for you. Hurry up, you haven't got all night. (Clive puts on wig and sunglasses. He has his back to the audience, looking at himself in a mirror. He turns to face the audience)
CLIVE	I'm not doing it, I'll look a right prat.
JACK	(Unconvincingly) You've just lost ten years in as many seconds.
CLIVE	I look like Elvis on a bad day.
JACK	That's still better than you on a good one. Trust me, have I ever let you down?
CLIVE	Well if you're sure.
JACK	Go for it, boy. You're just about to relive those swinging sixties.
CLIVE	I'd better put the kettle on, ready for my first date.

(Clive exits to kitchen)

JACK	(Shouting to Clive) Best of luck, (aside) you're going to need it. (Jack exits to hall. Clive enters from kitchen. He has another look in the mirror. He adjusts his wig and sunglasses. The doorbell rings, he exits to hall)
ANNABEL	(Off) Hello, my name is Annabel. (Entering from hall with Clive) Did your son tell you he's asked me round for a date? (Annabel puts her coat and bag on the sofa)
CLIVE	I'm your date tonight. It was me you spoke to.
ANNABEL	(Looking shocked) But you said on the phone you were thirty-five.

CLIVE I said I was slightly over thirty-five.

ANNABEL How much slightly over are you?

CLIVE Look, it's not important how old you are, it's how old you feel. (Pause) Would you like a coffee?

ANNABEL I'm not sure. (*Pause*) Oh all right I'll have one.

CLIVE Won't be a minute. (*Clive exits to kitchen. Annabel looks awkward, she picks up her coat and bag and tiptoes to hall exit just as Clive enters from kitchen with two cups of coffee*) Here you are.

ANNABEL Good grief, that was quick.

CLIVE (*Sensuously*) How do you like it? (*Handing over coffee*) With or without sugar?

ANNABEL (*Putting coat and bag on chair*) No sugar, thanks. (*Pause*) You remind me of someone and I just can't think who. (*Looking thoughtful*) I've got it, you look like Roy Orbison.

CLIVE Do you think so? I suppose you're one of his fans?

ANNABEL You must be joking. Although, my mum thinks he's great, she's got his photos all over our house.

CLIVE Actually, I'm not into all these past legends. I like to keep up with the modern stuff.

ANNABEL What do you think of Indi music?

CLIVE (*Looking vague*) I suppose it's all right for the Indians.

ANNABEL Have you been to any raves lately?

CLIVE (*Looking vague*) Sorry?

ANNABEL You know, the rave parties. The last one I went to kept going all weekend.

CLIVE I'll have you know you're talking to the king of Rock 'n' Roll. I can jive the night away with the best of them.

ANNABEL Jive? Whatever's that? (*Picking up a forty-five record*) Cor blimey. You're as bad as my mum, she's got a load of these old records.

CLIVE That one's a sixties classic, it's "Gerry and the Pacemakers."

ANNABEL Is this "Geriatric with his pacemaker" still alive?

CLIVE (*Getting cross*) Yes, and he's just completed a very successful world tour.

ANNABEL Don't tell me you've got one of those wind up gramophones. (*Bending over to have a close look at record player*) Where do you stick the handle?

CLIVE (*Aside- looking at Annabel's bottom*) Don't tempt me, or I may just tell you.

ANNABEL It's a bit like a museum in here, with all this old junk.

CLIVE (*Getting cross*) So what do you do when you're not at rave parties or looking round museums?

ANNABEL My boyfriend's got this boring hobby, at which he expects my unwavering support.

CLIVE You didn't tell me you had a boyfriend. (*Pause*) So what's his hobby, philately?

ANNABEL No, he's not one of them poofy dancers. He's the amateur bodybuilding champion of Southern England.

CLIVE Good grief, you're not thinking of telling him about me, are you?

ANNABEL I'm not stupid. If I did he'd finish with me, (*pause*) after he'd killed you. I've got a photo of him, here have a look. (*Annabel hands over a photo. Clive stares in disbelief*)

CLIVE He's certainly a big boy. Why's he got that iron bar round his neck?

ANNABEL He was showing off in front of the camera. He bent it just as I was taking his photo.

CLIVE He seems to have ripped his shirt.

ANNABEL That was caused by his bulging biceps. He's a very virile person. (*Sensuously*) It's all action when we get to bed.

CLIVE I souldn't think there's any room for you once he's in it.

ANNABEL (*Grabbing photo*) He's always treated me like a real lady.

CLIVE If you're so happy with Mr. Adonis, why put an advert in the lonely hearts?

ANNABEL I just fancied a bit of a laugh. (*Aside*) It's a pity things didn't work out.

(*The telephone rings. Clive answers it*)

CLIVE Hello ... Oh Jack, thank God, you've probably just saved my life ... Right I'll be straight round. (*Replaces receiver*) I'm sorry but I've got to go out.

ANNABEL Whatever's wrong?

CLIVE My mate's wife's having a baby, they need a lift to the hospital. I said I'd take them.

ANNABEL Oh right, I'd better go then. (*Annabel gets her coat and handbag*) I've just had a brilliant idea. (*Writing down phone number*) Why don't you give my mum a ring? You two have got a lot in common. (*Handing over piece of paper*) Here's her phone number. Bye. (*Annabel exits to hall*)

CLIVE Bye. (*Clive throws piece of paper in the bin. Then takes the two coffee cups to kitchen. He returns and sits on the sofa. The doorbell rings. Clive exits to hall - off*) Hello, come in. (*Clive enters from hall followed by Mavis*)

MAVIS Thank you for replying to my advert. I always welcome the opportunity of meeting new clients.

CLIVE I beg your pardon?

MAVIS I'm afraid I've told a little white lie. (*Getting close to Clive*) You see I'm here in a professional capacity.

CLIVE	You're a bit old to be on the game, aren't you?
MAVIS	(*Walking away from Clive*) No, you don't understand – I'm here to promote a brand new product. I've never felt better since I've been on the pill.
CLIVE	What are you on about?
MAVIS	I'm your local agent for a new wonder pill called "Super-Vit."
CLIVE	And what's that got to do with the lonely hearts adverts?
MAVIS	Placing the adverts gives me a way of meeting prospective customers.
CLIVE	So you're not looking for a date?
MAVIS	(*Getting out several bottles of pills and spreading them all over the table*) No, I'm here to show you my wares.
CLIVE	(*Getting angry*) That's not the sort of wares I was hoping to get a look at. (*Pause*) I could do you under the Trades Description Act. Your advert said you'd found the secret of life.
MAVIS	Exactly, and here it is. (*Holding up a bottle of pills*) You see, in the darkest African jungles, scientists have discovered they can extract a healing nutrient from plants which have been contaminated by monkey droppings.
CLIVE	But I'm looking for love and romance, not a bottle of monkey crap.
MAVIS	The properties found in these tablets can help with almost any eventuality.
CLIVE	How about being bitterly disappointed with the outcome of a date?
MAVIS	Do you find you're gasping for breath after making love?
CLIVE	Chance'd be a fine thing.

MAVIS (*Holding up another bottle of pills*) Two of these blue pills will soon get little Percy ready for action again. (*Pause*) Are you worried about age? Tired of looking at that wrinkled old face? (*Holding up another bottle of pills*) Try two of the red ones. (*Pause*) Although in your case, it might pay to double the dose.

CLIVE (*Looking at watch*) Look, I don't wish to be rude or hurt your feelings but as far as I'm concerned you can stuff those pills where the monkey stuffs his nuts.

MAVIS There's no need to be like that. (*Mavis opens a bottle, and takes a pill. Sitting on the sofa*) Do you have a wide circle of friends? (*Enthusiastically*) If you place a bulk order tonight, you'll be in line for an introductory offer discount.

CLIVE I don't know what I've got to do to convince you, I don't want your "Super-Vit pills." I'm not interested in the red ones, blue ones, or any other colours of the rainbow you might have. (*The telephone rings, Clive answers it*) Hello … Right, I'll be straight round … Bye. (*Replaces receiver*) I'm sorry, I've got to go out.

MAVIS But I've not shown you the portfolio yet. It explains how they extract the droppings from the contaminated plants. (*Clive gathers up the bottles of pills, and puts them back into Mavis's bag*)

CLIVE To be quite honest. I couldn't give a monkey's how they do it.

MAVIS (*Getting portfolio out*) It won't take me long, surely you've got a few minutes?

CLIVE My friend's wife is just about to give birth because she wasn't on the pill, and I've got to drive her to the hospital.

MAVIS Is it a breach?

CLIVE No it's a baby, and it won't wait while you and I are stood here talking. (*Clive puts portfolio away*)

MAVIS I'd better come with you, it's the least I can do. I used to be a midwife before I became an agent for "Super-Vit."

CLIVE I don't believe it. Why couldn't you have been a brickie's labourer or a steeplejack?

MAVIS I've brought many a child into the world. It'll be nice to get my hand in again.

CLIVE It's all right, her own GP's meeting us at the hospital. In any case she's very shy where strangers are concerned. (*Pushing Mavis towards the door*)

MAVIS After twenty-four hours in labour I used to find that all inhibitions disappeared. (*Pause*) I'll tell you what, borrow these "Super-Vit" energy pills. She's going to need them. Goodbye. (*Mavis hands over pills then exits to hall. Clive puts pills on shelf, then dials number on phone*)

CLIVE Hello, Jack, it's me … Don't ask, it's turning out to be a total disaster … Don't leave it any longer than five minutes, the next one will probably be a bloke … Bye.

(*Replaces receiver then removes wig and sunglasses. He puts a record on of The Hollies singing "He Ain't Heavy, He's My Brother." The doorbell rings. Clive exits to hall*)

EMILY (*Off*) Hello, I hope I'm not too early.

CLIVE (*Off*) No, please come in. (Clive and Emily enter)

EMILY That's one of my all time favourite records. I love the sounds of the sixties.

CLIVE I know it sounds corny, but they don't make records like that nowadays. (*Turns the music down*)

EMILY I didn't know whether to come tonight. You see, I've never done anything like this before.

CLIVE I'm so glad you did. Would you like a drink?

EMILY Could I have an orange juice, please? (*Clive pours out two orange juices*)

CLIVE You can have anything you want.

EMILY (*Getting embarrassed*) Thank you.

CLIVE	} Have you lived …?
EMILY	} What made you …? I'm sorry, you first.
CLIVE	Have you lived round here long?
EMILY	No. My father died when I was young, and after nursing my mother through a long illness, she sadly passed away. (*With sadness*) So I decided it was time to move on.
CLIVE	I'm so pleased. (*Getting flustered*) I mean, I'm very sorry to hear about your parents, but I'm glad you moved here.

(*Clive hands over orange juice. They make eye contact for a lingering second*)

	Cheers.
EMILY	Cheers. (*Pause*) I'm a very shy person, and I've been using my mother's illness as an excuse not to go out and enjoy myself.
CLIVE	Well all that's going to change now you're here. I've prepared a special meal for us tonight.
EMILY	I never realised I'd be dining out with an experienced chef. (*The telephone rings*)
CLIVE	Excuse me. (*Clive picks up receiver*) Hello … Oh, hello, Jack …Right … I'll take her tomorrow … Well, tell her to cross her legs … Bye (*Replaces receiver*)
EMILY	Have you got to go somewhere?
CLIVE	No, the night is ours, it's just you, me and the sixties.
EMILY	And this special meal of yours.
CLIVE	Oh yes, I'll just check it's all coming together.
EMILY	Can I have a look? I love to watch an experienced cook at work, I might learn something.

CLIVE　　Best not to spoil things, I want it to be a surprise. (*Clive exits to kitchen. Emily starts looking through the records. Clive enters from kitchen looking at watch*) About another four minutes should do it.

EMILY　　You've got some lovely records here.

(*Clive joins Emily. They look through records together*)

CLIVE　　If you've any favourites, we'll listen to them.

EMILY　　Wouldn't it be sad if there wasn't any music in our lives?

CLIVE　　I'd never really thought about it. (*Looking into Emily's eyes*) I suppose it's like most things, unless you've experienced the pleasure of it, you don't know what you're missing. (*Clive goes to put his arm around Emily*)

EMILY　　Could I have another drink, please? It's getting rather warm in here.

CLIVE　　Certainly, one orange juice coming up. (*Clive pours out drink*)

EMILY　　So what made you reply to my advert?

CLIVE　　I decided it was time to bring some life back into my life. Does that make any sense?

EMILY　　A great deal. (*Clive hands drink to Emily*) Thank you. (*Pause*) I seem to spend all my time worrying about unimportant things, instead of enjoying the moment.

CLIVE　　Life is so precious, we shouldn't waste a minute. (*Clive goes to put his arm around Emily. The phone rings*) Excuse me.

EMILY　　I don't think I've locked my car. I'll just check. (*Emily exits to hall. Clive picks up receiver*)

CLIVE　　(*Shouting to Emily*) See you in a sec. (*Speaking into phone*) ... Hello ... Ah... hello, dear ... Yes, (*unconvincingly*) I was ... um ... just talking to, Jack ... Right, I'll feed the fish, hang on a minute. (*Clive puts receiver down, and feeds the fish with the "Super-Vit*

	pills") Just keep your mouth shut, Suzie. (*Then returns to phone*) I've done it ... Yes, I've done that ... And that ... Yes, dear ... Yes, dear, No, dear, (*aside*) three bags full, dear... Right, see you tomorrow. (*Replaces receiver. Emily enters*)
EMILY	What a lovely evening, so peaceful and still.
CLIVE	If only life could be like that all the time.
EMILY	I know so little about you, and yet I feel completely at ease when we're together.
CLIVE	I've never met a girl like you before. Where have you been all my life? (*Clive puts his arm around Emily. The doorbell rings*) Oh no, please excuse me. (*Clive exits to hall*)
HENRY	(*Off*) Hello, I'm from the local paper. (*Henry enters from hall. He is carrying a large case, which he puts on the table. Clive follows him into room*)
CLIVE	I'm sorry, but what are you doing here? (*Henry opens his case*)
HENRY	How rude of me. Henry Clark's the name. (*Handing over a business card from the case*) I'm here to take a few photos of the happy couple.
CLIVE	What are you talking about?
HENRY	(*Getting a piece of paper from case*) You are Mr. Clive Debanks, of 56 Malom Way? And you did reply to an advert in the local paper?
CLIVE	(*Looking totally confused*) Well, yes, but I still don't understand.
HENRY	(*Getting Polaroid camera out of case, and opening a notebook*) Surely, you must have realised we'd be checking on the details.
CLIVE	I've never done anything like this before.
HENRY	It's surprising how many people tell porky pies.

EMILY Porky pies?

HENRY Lies!! I like to catch people when they least expect me. You get a true picture of the couple then.

CLIVE Well, you've certainly caught us unexpectedly. (*Henry starts to make notes in his notebook*)

HENRY This is all very romantic. A candlelit meal. The couple are smartly dressed, not sat in front of the telly.

EMILY So you're saying this is normal procedure when people reply to the advert?

HENRY Most certainly. How else do you think we could tell whether your relationship is a success?

CLIVE (*Totally confused*) I didn't realise it would involve all this.

HENRY (*Still writing in notebook*) I've just been listening through your letterbox to see if you were rowing.

EMILY But surely we're entitled to some privacy.

HENRY Not when you reply to an advert in our paper. (*Holding Polaroid camera*) Right, I just need a couple of photos, then I'll be out of your way.

CLIVE Hang on a minute, I'm not so sure about this.

HENRY Look, I've had a long day and I'm feeling a bit cream crackered.

EMILY Sorry?

HENRY Knackered!! I can assure you we exercise complete discretion, it's purely for our records. So could you please hold hands?

EMILY (*To Clive*) I'm happy to do it if you are. (*Getting hold of Clive's hand – to Henry*) Is this all right?

HENRY Oh very nice, and may I say what a lovely couple you make. (*Henry takes a photo*) One more, arm in arm. (*Emily gets hold of Clive's arm*) That's wonderful. (*Clive*

	looks awkward as Henry takes photo) And finally I'll just need one of the happy couple kissing.
CLIVE	} Kissing?
EMILY	} Kissing?
HENRY	Don't tell me you're both shy, after all these years.
CLIVE	Of course I'm not, but that's hardly the point.
HENRY	I've got several other couples to visit tonight. So if you wouldn't mind getting on with it.
CLIVE	(*Looking at Emily*) It's up to you.
EMILY	Oh, why not, after all he's only doing his job.
HENRY	Right, if you'd look into each others mince pies.
EMILY	Pardon?
HENRY	Eyes!! Could we have eye contact please. (*Clive and Emily look into each others eyes. They start kissing passionately. Henry takes a photo of them*) Now we're getting somewhere.
CLIVE	(*Breaking off kiss for a second*) You can say that again. (*Clive gives Emily another passionate kiss*)
HENRY	That's it, I'm all done. (*Getting close to the kissing couple*) I've finished. (*Henry puts all his things back into the case, as the kiss continues*) Still enjoys kissing after twenty-eight years of marriage. That's amazing. (*Emily and Clive are oblivious of Henry's remarks*) I must be off. (*Walking to hall exit, carrying his case*) From what I've seen here today, you're in with an excellent chance of winning the competition. (*Henry exits to hall. The kiss continues. The microwave bell rings*)

Scene III
As the curtain rises, Tracy is pacing up and down the room. Anita is sitting on the sofa, and Claire is sitting on a chair. Tracy's suitcase is on the table. (Suggestion - Suzie the goldfish could be twice the size after eating the 'Super–Vit' pills)

TRACY	You said you'd sort things out, Mum. You said you'd make him see sense.
ANITA	Well, I do deserve some credit. At least he's not going to be one of those hippies.
TRACY	(*Getting cross*) Oh, that's very reassuring, considering he's just announced we'll be joining the Hells Angels.
CLAIRE	If he was approaching middle age, you could put it down to the male menopause, but he's too young for the midlife crisis.
TRACY	(*With distress*) I can't get my head round all this.
CLAIRE	I wonder what chapter you'll be in. (*Pause*) It was on telly the other night. When you join the Hells Angels they put you into a chapter. It's so you know who to go round bashing up.
TRACY	He's even suggested me having a "Harley Davidson" tattooed across my chest.
ANITA	I dread to ask where the wheels'll be going.
TRACY	We should have started a family. That would have made him more responsible.
ANITA	I'm not so sure about that. Most of the responsibility in bringing up the kids is down to the woman.
CLAIRE	All men have to do is grunt and groan for a couple of minutes and then it's over to us for the next nine months.
ANITA	We even have to double up as a mobile canteen. And once the teeth arrive we should get danger money. Plus the fact we're deprived of sleep for the next few years.
TRACY	When Tom asked me to marry him, he said we'd be living in the fast lane. I didn't think that meant on the back of a flaming motorbike. Do you think he'll ever come to his senses, and realise he belongs in the rat race with the rest of us?
ANITA	He's obviously going through some sort of identity crisis.

CLAIRE	(*Reassuringly*) These things have a way of working themselves out. I'm sure you'll soon come up with a simple answer.
TRACY	You could be right. (*Pause*) How do I start divorce proceedings?
ANITA	That's a bit hasty. Don't do anything we might all live to regret.
CLAIRE	I didn't realise you thought so much of your son-in-law.
ANITA	Actually I was more concerned it might ruin my chance of a Caribbean cruise.
CLAIRE	Of course, you're trying to convince the competition judges that you're all one big happy family.
ANITA	I'm surprised they haven't been in touch, or at least taken our photo.
CLAIRE	Have you told Clive anything about it yet?
ANITA	No, I'm leaving that till the last minute, I don't want him messing things up.
TRACY	Mum, instead of worrying about some Caribbean cruise, could we please sort out my marriage?
ANITA	I'm sorry. It's just that after twenty-eight years, I feel I'm entitled to some reward.
CLAIRE	(*To Anita*) I've not seen much of Clive lately. Where's he been hiding?
ANITA	He's been spending all his time at the Nag's Head, helping the landlord set up a new karaoke player.
CLAIRE	I'm surprised he's not taken up bowls, it seems to turn most middle aged men on.
TRACY	(*Shouting*) Look, I'm just about to become a tattooed leather-clad biker, travelling the towns in search of a punch-up. Could someone please help me?

ANITA You've probably been too soft on the boy. Once they get above themselves you've had it.

TRACY You're right, Mum, he's been taking me for granted. If he wants our marriage to survive he's got to toe-the-line. I'm certainly not crawling back to him. (*Doorbell rings*)

ANITA That's probably him now, frightened to come in.

TRACY Oh, Mum, he's realised his mistakes. (*Running to hall exit*) I forgive you, my darling. (*Tracy exits – off*) Oh, hello, can I help you?

MAVIS (*Entering from hall followed by Tracy*) I've called to collect my bottle of pills.

ANITA You're obviously lost. The building you want is full of wines and spirits, with a large sign above the door saying "Off licence."

MAVIS No, you don't understand. I've called to collect my "Super-Vit" tablets which I left the other night.

ANITA I haven't got a clue what you're on about.

MAVIS (*Looking at Tracy*) And you must be the proud mother. Congratulations. (*Shaking Tracy's hand*) I did offer to help. (*Pause*) So what sex did you have?

TRACY (*Totally confused*) I beg your pardon?

MAVIS I used to be a midwife many years ago. After the birth, I insisted that the mother stopped screaming or using foul language before I'd tell her what she'd had.

ANITA (*Aside – to Claire*) She must be a fruit and nut case.

MAVIS (*Looking around the room - getting cross*) I must have my bottle of pills, we have to account for every tablet. I did make it clear to the gentleman that he could have a few tablets, as a goodwill gesture. (*Walking over to Anita and having a good look at her*) Isn't the diet working?

ANITA How dare you. Are you suggesting I'm overweight?

MAVIS	I bet you used to laugh when people mentioned liposuction, but I guess now you're seriously looking at the cost?
ANITA	I've heard enough of this. Would you kindly leave?
MAVIS	Have you ever seen a fat monkey?
ANITA	(*Aside - to Claire*) You've got to do something. She's lost the plot.
MAVIS	You don't have to suffer in silence. "Super-Vit" will solve all your problems. (*Walking over to Tracy*) Does your husband take you for granted?
TRACY	Yes, he does, how did you know?
MAVIS	It's always the same after childbirth, when your body's not as firm as it used to be.
TRACY	(*Indignantly*) There's nothing wrong with my body.
MAVIS	Some husbands feel rejected, they think the baby's encroaching on their territory.
TRACY	What baby are you talking about?
MAVIS	(*Walking over to Anita*) That's a bad sign, she's already rejecting the little one.
CLAIRE	I really think it's time you went. (*Putting her arm on Mavis' shoulder*) There's probably lots more babies just waiting for you to bring them into the world.
MAVIS	I'm not a midwife. I packed all that in years ago, when I realised that "Super-Vit" was the miracle drug we'd all been waiting for. (*Picking up bottle of pills from behind goldfish bowl*) Ah, here they are.
ANITA	(*Looking at bottle of pills in amazement*) I don't believe it. (*Forcefully*) Right, now would you please leave?
MAVIS	Are you sure you wouldn't like to see our full range of "Super-Vit" pills? They'll cure anything from panic attacks to piles.

ANITA No thank you. Goodbye.

MAVIS Oh, all right, I'll see myself out. Bye. (*Mavis exits to hall, then pops her head back into room*) Don't forget, when it comes to feeding, breast is best. (*Mavis exits to hall*)

ANITA Am I going round the twist, or did some demented woman just come in here and remove a bottle of pills from my shelf?

CLAIRE There must be a simple explanation. She could be one of those door to door sales people.

ANITA You're probably right, and knowing my husband, he'd get sucked in like a lemon, and wouldn't be able to get rid of her.

CLAIRE So what made her keep on about delivering babies?

TRACY (*Starting to cry*) I couldn't care less why she kept on about babies, or "Super-Vit" pills. My marriage is on the rocks, what am I going to do?

ANITA There's only one thing you can do. Move back in here until the moron comes to his senses.

TRACY (*Stops crying*) I'll pack my things away. (*Looking at Suzie*) Suzie looks pregnant. (*Tracy exits to hall carrying her suitcase*)

CLAIRE It'll be quite like old times having your daughter back home.

ANITA Thank goodness our son's emigrated or we could be playing happy families again.

CLAIRE I might find myself another partner. I miss having a man around.

ANITA (*The phone rings. Anita answers it*) Hello … Oh it's you, I'll see if she wants to talk. (*Anita puts the phone down and exits to hall – off*) Tracy, it's your husband. (*Anita enters, followed by Tracy, who picks up receiver*)

TRACY (*Shouting*) Are you kneeling down? … You're not, right… (*Tracy slams receiver down*)

CLAIRE Any progress in the reconciliation? (*The phone rings, Tracy answers it*)

TRACY (*Shouting*) Are you on bended knee? … In that case you may speak … I've heard enough. (*Tracy slams receiver down*)

CLAIRE It's nice to hear that things are moving forward just a little bit.

(*The phone rings, Tracy answers it*)

TRACY (*Shouting*) Are you still kneeling down? … Right, you'll be getting a list of my demands by the next post … Goodbye, and don't ring back. (*Tracy slams down receiver, then leaves it off the hook*) If he calls round, tell him I've gone out. (*Exits to hall*)

ANITA I'll pass the message on.

CLAIRE Have you decided what you're getting Clive for his fiftieth?

ANITA It's a toss up between a C.D. player and a washing machine.

CLAIRE Surely, a washing machine's not a very personal present.

ANITA It'll be used to wash all his smelly socks and dirty old pants. You can't get any more personal than that.

(*Doorbell rings*)

Would you go, Claire? If it's that travelling sales person, get rid of her. (*Claire exits to hall*)

CLAIRE (*Off*) Hello, Jack, come in. (*Jack and Claire enter*)

JACK Hello, isn't he back yet? I arranged to meet him here at four.

ANITA	I thought you were both at the pub, checking the karaoke equipment.
JACK	(*Looking vague*) Sorry?
CLAIRE	How's it you've never married, Jack? You must be the most eligible bachelor around.
JACK	I guess I've never found the right girl.
CLAIRE	(*Getting close to Jack*) You don't know what you're missing.
JACK	(*Looking at Anita*) I've got a pretty good idea.
CLAIRE	Sometimes you can overlook what's on offer right under your nose.
JACK	I'll surprise you all one day, just wait and see.
CLAIRE	(*Sensuously*) Don't leave it too long, us girls don't wait for ever.
JACK	When the time's right, I'll be handing out the presents and writing the romantic messages.
CLAIRE	I'll look forward to that.

(*Jack is completely oblivious to Claire's advances. Clive enters from hall*)

CLIVE	Hello, all.
ANITA	I hope you've got a very good explanation.
CLIVE	(*Looking very worried*) What for?
ANITA	Your daughter's moving back here because the husband, you said was the catch of the century, has just become a Hell's Angel.
CLIVE	(*Looking relieved*) Oh, is that all? I mean, leave them to it, they'll work things out.
ANITA	It's obvious we are not getting anywhere down here. Let's help Tracy get her room ready.

CLAIRE	(*Sensuously*) See you in a minute, Jack. (*Claire smiles at Jack, then exits with Anita to hall. Jack walks over to hall exit to make sure they've gone, then returns into room. He then looks at Clive's neck*)
JACK	Three weeks, no love bite. It's payout time.
CLIVE	Do you believe in love at first sight? (*With sincerity*) I've just met a girl I can't live without.
JACK	A man of your age can't fall in love. It's a physical impossibility.
CLIVE	In my wildest dreams, I'd never realised such feelings existed. Emily's turned my whole world upside down.
JACK	She was the last of your dates, wasn't she?
CLIVE	Yes, and the moment she walked through the door, I knew there was something special about her.
JACK	It's all dropping into place now. For the past three weeks I've hardly seen you, and when we've been together you've been on another planet.
CLIVE	Emily's not like any other girl I've ever met before.
JACK	So what are you saying, she's got some extra bits and pieces?
CLIVE	No, I mean when I'm with her, the feelings of passion are incredible. She's the most warm-hearted, affectionate woman I've ever known.
JACK	You told me you were after a bit of slap and tickle, not a full blown affair.

(*Clive and Jack sit on sofa*)

CLIVE	I didn't go looking for it, but from the moment our eyes met, the chemistry just took over. She's rekindled all my lost emotions.
JACK	I'm very pleased for you. (*Pause*) Look, you've had your bit of fun but now it's back to reality. You're a married man.

CLIVE You're absolutely right and, in fairness to my wife, I should tell her all about it.

JACK That's probably not the best idea you've ever had. Assuming you want to carry on living.

CLIVE I'm not living without Emily, we were made for each other. (*With sincerity*) My marriage is over.

JACK So you're prepared to sacrifice twenty-eight years of wedded bliss, a semi-detached house with fixtures and fittings, the family car and Suzie the goldfish, for a girl you met only three weeks ago?

CLIVE Emily's not just any girl. When we're together the world has some meaning. We can talk for hours, or sit in silence just holding each other. For the first time in years I feel alive.

(*Clive stares into space in a dream. He puts his hand on Jack's knee. Jack removes it*)

JACK You wouldn't be making up this story because she won't give you a love bite?

CLIVE If only my life were that simple. I'm in love with one woman and married to another.

JACK That's no different than half the male population of the world.

CLIVE Whatever am I going to do?

JACK (*Looking thoughtful*) Tomorrow we'll go to the animal rescue sanctuary and get you man's best friend, a dog.

CLIVE My marriage is a farce. I'm hopelessly in love with another woman and your best suggestion is to get a pet.

JACK With a dog it's possible to keep your girl friend and wife.

CLIVE How can a canine colleague solve my infidelity dilemma?

JACK When you want to ring your girlfriend, take the dog out for a walk.

CLIVE I hadn't thought of that.

JACK You've had lunch with your girlfriend, you get home to a big meal, give it to the dog.

CLIVE I hadn't thought of that.

JACK You've been out with your girlfriend, you're smelling of her perfume. Get the dog to give you a good licking.

CLIVE I hadn't thought of that. (*Pause*) Hang on a minute, the vicar's got four dogs.

JACK That explains why he always looks knackered.

CLIVE Everything's getting so complicated, I can't live a life of lies and deceit.

JACK It goes with the territory, unless you give up this love goddess.

CLIVE No, Emily means everything to me. I'm not giving her up. I'm leaving my wife.

JACK (*Getting serious*) Now you listen to me. You've been tasting forbidden fruits. This is very serious stuff.

CLIVE Don't you think I know that? But Emily's the best thing that's ever happened to me. (*Pause*) I've wasted the best part of my life, having never experienced true love. But now that I have, I'm certainly not giving it up.

JACK And is this wonder woman single?

CLIVE Yes, she's been nursing her sick mother and yes she knows I'm married. But that's soon going to change.

JACK Just keep your options open for now. It's early days yet.

(*Clive hands Jack a box and card*)

CLIVE I bought her a necklace. Look. I've had a C for Clive engraved on it, to remind her of me.

JACK You must want your head examined. (*Jack studies necklace and looks at card. Claire enters from hall, unseen by Jack or Clive. Jack reads aloud from card*) To the one and only true love in my life.

CLAIRE Who are you talking about?

JACK (*Turning round and looking startled*) Oh, Claire, it's you. I mean, I didn't realize you were …

CLAIRE So, I'm the girl you're going to surprise with presents and romantic messages?

JACK No … you don't understand … (*Looking at Clive*) I don't know what to say.

CLAIRE Oh, Jack, don't be embarrassed, you dear man. (*Claire gives Jack a kiss, and takes the necklace*) It's absolutely beautiful, thank you so much. (*Looking at necklace*) You've even thought to put a C for Claire on it.

JACK Good grief, what have I done?

CLAIRE You've just made me the happiest girl in the world.

CLIVE (*Aside*) That's fifty quid down the drain.

CLAIRE And what a lovely message. Do you mind if I go and show the others?

JACK (*Looking totally fed up*) Not at all, be my guest. (*Claire gives Jack another kiss and exits to hall*)

CLIVE What the hell are you playing at?

JACK Don't blame me, I got you off the hook and got myself well and truly on it. Now I'm completely lumbered. (*The doorbell rings. Clive exits to hall*)

CLIVE (*Off*) Oh, hello. (*Henry enters from hall with a camera round his neck. He has three photos in his hand. Clive follows him in*)

HENRY I've been trying to get you on the dog and bone.

CLIVE	Pardon?
HENRY	The phone. But someone's left it off the hook. (*Henry replaces receiver*)
CLIVE	What are you doing here, can't you leave me alone?
HENRY	I must say that's not very nice, especially considering I'm the bearer of good news. (*Shaking Clive's hand*) Congratulations. You've made it through to the last eight.
CLIVE	Oh, that's great. (*Pause*) The last eight what?
HENRY	The boy's a comedian. Eight couples are through to the semi-final of "Mr. & Mrs. Perfect Marriage" and you're one of them.
CLIVE	(*Looking vague*) I didn't even realise we'd entered.
HENRY	You're just a laugh a minute. It was the candlelight supper that convinced me. I've never seen such a perfect couple. (*Tracy, Anita and Claire enter from the hall. Claire is wearing the necklace*)
CLAIRE	Thank you so much Jack, I love it.
HENRY	Hello, ladies, you could be standing next to the dog's dinner.
TRACY	I beg your pardon?
HENRY	The winner! (*Looking at Tracy*) Is this your daughter?
CLIVE	Yes.
HENRY	(*To Tracy*) Your mum and dad have just made it through to the last round of "Mr. & Mrs. Perfect Marriage." (*Henry hands round the photos*) I can't stop, I'm visiting the other semi-finalists. I'd love to see your wife's face when you tell her. Still, I suppose the photos say it all. (*Henry exits to hall. Anita looks at photo. Her face turns to rage*)

Blackout

ACT II
Scene I

As the curtain rises the stage is empty and the phone is ringing. Anita enters from kitchen and answers it.

ANITA Hello … Yes, this is Anita Debanks … No, we haven't received any notification …. What? … So you'll be here in twenty minutes … But my husband's gone out … Hello… Hello … Hello. (Replaces receiver) I don't believe it. (*The doorbell rings. Anita exits to hall - off*) Claire, Jack, come in.

(Claire, Jack and Anita enter from hall. Claire is all over Jack, he keeps moving away)

CLAIRE Jack's just taken me out to lunch. I'm so full I can hardly move.

JACK That's hardly surprising considering, after polishing off your own meal, you got stuck into all my leftovers.

CLAIRE Oh, Jack, you don't think I acted like a pig, do you?

JACK No, of course you didn't. (*Aside*) Pigs don't grunt as loud as you.

ANITA (*With urgency*) The competition people have just rung, they're sending a car round in fifteen minutes to pick Clive and me up. Apparently we should have received a letter saying we've made it through to the final three couples.

CLAIRE Congratulations. That's wonderful news. (*Claire gives Anita a kiss*)

ANITA They're making the final choice this afternoon.

JACK I'm very pleased for you and Clive. (*Jack shakes Anita's hand*)

ANITA It's no thanks to my stupid husband. (*Getting cross*) If it wasn't for him, we wouldn't be in the predicament we are.

CLAIRE	What predicament?
ANITA	(*Picking up photos*) If you remember, all the romantic photos on which the judges based their verdict are of my husband with some phantom woman. (*Anita hands photos to Claire*)
CLAIRE	Oh dear, I'd forgotten about these.
JACK	Clive has explained what happened. (*Unconvincingly*) She was his partner in the Karaoke competition. He'd asked you to go, but you refused.
ANITA	I certainly wasn't making a fool of myself in front of a pub full of lager louts.
JACK	That's why he had to search around for a girl to form a double act.
CLAIRE	I still don't understand why they came back here, and let the photographer take a picture of them kissing.
JACK	(*Unconvincingly*) Clive told you. They were impersonating Peters and Lee, so he needed his sunglasses. They'd just got here, when the competition photographer arrived.
CLAIRE	Of course you hadn't told Clive anything about the wedding competition.
JACK	Exactly. (*With confidence*) So he assumed it was something to do with the Karaoke competition. And reluctantly, he posed with the girl.
ANITA	I suppose it does all make sense.
CLAIRE	The only other explanation would be if Clive was having an affair. (*Claire and Anita start to laugh. Jack fiddles about with his collar and looks awkward*)
ANITA	Well, now you put it like that, his story must be true, no woman would ever fall for my husband. (*Anita and Claire continue laughing*)

CLAIRE	Unless he's got something to offer the girls you're not telling us about.
ANITA	You must be joking.
CLAIRE	So what are you going to do about the competition? It's the opportunity of a lifetime.
ANITA	If only they hadn't taken these photos.
JACK	Let me have a look at them. (*Jack examines photos*) These were taken with a Polaroid camera.
ANITA	It doesn't matter what camera took them. What does matter is the wrong woman's on them.
JACK	No, you're missing the point, with a Polaroid camera there aren't any negatives. So all we've got to do is destroy these photos and substitute them for three which we'll take of you and Clive.
CLAIRE	I get it, no negatives, no proof.
JACK	That's right, we've got the only photos taken. Now all we need is a Polaroid camera so we can take some more.
CLAIRE	I've got one at home. You used it the other night, to take all those naughty photos of me in the bedroom. (*Holding Jack's arm*) You said I was your little centrefold.
JACK	(*Looking embarrassed*) Oh yes, and there's still plenty of film left.
CLAIRE	That's only because you'd lost interest in taking photos and started …
JACK	All right, I don't think we need to paint a picture of what happened.
ANITA	There's just one more fly in the ointment, my husband's done one of his disappearing acts.
JACK	He's probably in the pub. (*Jack crosses his fingers and holds them behind his back*) I'll go and find him while you two are getting the camera. (*Pause*) I suggest we

	put some family photos around the room. It'll help create the illusion of a happy marriage.
ANITA	That certainly is only an illusion. (*Opening the cupboard*) Here's the ones we normally drag out at family do's. (*Anita gets out the photos and hands them to Claire and Jack*) They've been dusted off ready for the birthday party tomorrow. (*They stand the photos around the room. Tracy enters from hall*) If by some miracle your dad arrives home, keep him here.
TRACY	Why, what's happening?
ANITA	(*Getting excited*) You could be looking at the winner of Mr. and Mrs. Perfect Marriage, we're a whisker away from a Caribbean cruise.
TRACY	(*Bursting into tears*) I hope you'll have a lovely time.
ANITA	Whatever's the matter?
TRACY	In case anybody hadn't noticed, my marriage is all but over. Whatever shall I do? (*Anita takes Tracy to one side*)
ANITA	Just don't say anything to the judges. It may ruin our chances.
TRACY	So what are you suggesting? I put on a nun's habit, so you can tell them I've taken a vow of silence. (*Tracy cries uncontrollably*) I want my husband back. Why doesn't he give me a ring?
ANITA	It's because he gave you a ring you've got all these problems.
JACK	We'd better go or we'll never be back in time.
ANITA	Goodbye, dear, and don't forget, a nice big smile when the man's here. We're all just one big happy family.

(*Anita, Jack and Claire exit to hall. Tracy keeps on snivelling. The phone rings. Tracy answers it*)

TRACY Hello … Oh, it's you, I thought I told you not to ring … (*Starting to cry*) Yes, I'd love to see you, but I'm not being a Hell's Angel … All right come round here and we'll have a talk … They're all going out this afternoon … See you soon … Bye.

(*Replaces receiver, then looks into mirror and adjusts her hair. She then exists to hall. After a few seconds Clive enters from hall. He goes to the phone and dials a number*)

CLIVE Hello, Emily … Thank you for a wonderful time … I love you so much, I can't bear it when we're apart … I've decided the minute my wife comes in, I'm telling her the marriage is over … Yes, I'm certain … Bye.

(*Replaces receiver, and walks around the room practising his lines aloud*)

You'd better sit down, we've got a small problem … Um … You know when we first got married and your mum said it wouldn't last? Well … Um … Don't get cross, (*Tracy enters room, unseen by Clive*) but I've got something to tell you that could make a slight difference to our lives.

TRACY What's that, Dad? (*Clive turns round looking startled*)

CLIVE Oh, Tracy, I didn't realise you were here. I was just thinking aloud.

TRACY Tom's on his way round. I need your advice, you've been married a long time. What's it like when you're deeply in love?

CLIVE What do you want to deal with first, the marriage, or being deeply in love?

TRACY Dad, I'm serious, would you please stop kidding about? All right, I know you've had your ups and downs, but you must be doing something right.

CLIVE For the last five weeks, even I don't know what I've been doing.

TRACY Well you can relax now, by the end of the day you could be the winners.

CLIVE	Winners of what?
TRACY	Hasn't anyone told you? You're going for an interview this afternoon. They've narrowed it down to three couples.
CLIVE	You mean we're still in that competition?
TRACY	Yes, they're making the final choice. You could soon be on your Caribbean cruise.
CLIVE	Tracy, we need to talk. Something very important's happened in my life. (*The doorbell rings*)
TRACY	I'll get it. (*Exits to hall – off*) Hello, Jack, come in. (*Tracy and Jack enter*)
JACK	Thank goodness you're back.
TRACY	Dad, we'll talk later. I need to work on my face, so my husband'll realise what he's been missing. (*Exits to hall*)
CLIVE	I should never have listened to you the other day. Everything would have been sorted out by now.
JACK	So you've still got the hots for wonder woman?
CLIVE	If you mean am I in love with Emily, the answer's yes and I'm just about to tell my wife our marriage is over.
JACK	I really don't think that's such a good idea, considering you're about to become a role model for aspiring husbands.
CLIVE	I just want to get things sorted out. If you were a real mate, you'd be helping me.
JACK	I am helping you. I'm keeping your competition hopes alive. It was me who suggested taking new photos (*Claire and Anita enter from hall. Anita is carrying a Polaroid camera*) to replace the ones of you with Emi… (*Jack sees Claire and Anita*). Everybody ready then?
ANITA	Thank goodness you're back. (*Getting cross*) Next time, don't disappear when you're wanted.

CLIVE	We need to have a very serious talk.	
ANITA	Don't be stupid, we've only got two minutes to take the photos. (*Anita hands over camera to Jack*)	
CLIVE	But this is very important, it's going to affect our lives together.	
ANITA	You're absolutely right, if we don't get these pictures correct, bang goes my chance of a Caribbean cruise. (*Anita looks at photo then grabs Clive*) Right, Jack, we're all ready – take it now. (*Anita looks at Clive*) Smile you idiot. (*Jack smiles*) Not you, Jack. I was talking to my stupid husband. (*Jack takes photo*)	
CLAIRE	One down, two to go.	
CLIVE	I've got something to say…	
ANITA	Just shut up, and do what you're told.	
CLAIRE	(*Looking at the photo*) On this one, you're arm in arm.	
ANITA	Come here, look into my eyes, and don't forget we're blissfully happy. (*Jack takes a picture*)	
JACK	Last one coming up.	
CLAIRE	You're kissing on this one.	
ANITA	What I have to do, to get on a Caribbean cruise. (*Anita grabs Clive's ear, pulls him into place and kisses him. Jack takes the photo*)	
CLIVE	(*Looking miserable*) Is that it?	
ANITA	For goodness sake, cheer up, anybody would think you're having a photo taken at your own funeral.	
JACK	(*Jack rips up the old photos*) Time to destroy the incriminating evidence.	
CLIVE	Would someone please listen to me?	

(*The doorbell rings*)

ANITA	(*To Clive*) Don't just stand there like a pregnant pig, answer the door.

(*Clive exits to hall*)

HENRY	(*Off*) You lucky chap. (*Henry and Clive enter. Henry is carrying a camera and tripod*) Right, one or two details to sort out here, and then it's into the jam jar.

ANITA	Sorry?

HENRY	The car. (*Walking over to Clive*) I'll be whisking you and your good lady wife off to the interview. Are you getting excited?

CLIVE	(*Unconvincingly*) Yea, I'm absolutely ecstatic.

HENRY	So where's your better half?

ANITA	I'm here.

HENRY	Sorry, (*To Clive*) I meant that gorgeous girl you were with the other night.

ANITA	That was me.

HENRY	There seems to be some confusion here. (*To Clive*) I'm looking for your trouble and strife.

ANITA	I may not be his trouble and strife but I'm certainly his wife.

HENRY	(*Looking confused*) But … you're …

ANITA	(*Handing over the photos*) Here's the three photos you took of us the other night. (*Henry studies the photos very carefully. He keeps looking at Anita then at the photos*)

HENRY	I don't understand this. (*Pause*) They say the camera never lies. It must have been the lighting.

CLAIRE	Is there a problem? I can vouch for this couple's authenticity.

HENRY No, everything's just fine. My wife's told me to get my mince pies checked. (*Pause*) I'd seen a lot of couples that day. (*Looking confused*) I've obviously got you mixed up with someone else.

JACK There's lots of family photos here, where they've shared those treasured moments together.

(*Jack guides Henry round the room*)

HENRY Oh yes, very nice, what a lovely couple.

JACK So when do they leave for the Caribbean cruise?

HENRY We're not quite there yet, sir. (*Pause*) Now I'd like a photo of you with your children.

ANITA Our son's emigrated, we miss him so much.

HENRY What about your lovely daughter, she'd popped round the other day. Could we contact her for a family photo?

ANITA Just by sheer coincidence, she's popped round here again today.

CLAIRE I'll give her a shout. (*Claire exits to hall – off*) Tracy, you're needed for a happy family photo. (*Claire enters room*)

HENRY And what about her husband, is he here? (*Clive takes Jack to one side and they start arguing*)

ANITA (*Unconvincingly*) I'm afraid Tom's been sent to Japan on a business trip. He's always travelling the world making executive decisions.

TRACY (*Entering from hall*) Tom's just phoned, he's on his way over.

HENRY Now that is good news, will he be here by tomorrow?

TRACY He'll be here in ten minutes, he's on his bike.

(*Henry looks totally confused*)

ANITA   How silly of me, of course he flew back yesterday, a day earlier than expected.

(*Clive and Jack are still arguing in the background*)

HENRY   I feel a photo coming on. I think I'll take some outside in the garden. (*Claire walks to kitchen exit*) Just of the family, if you don't mind.

CLAIRE   (*Looking disappointed*) Oh, right, we'll wait in here. (*Clive, Anita and Tracy exit to kitchen followed by Henry. Claire grabs Jack and pulls him onto the sofa*) Alone at last. (*Claire gives Jack a passionate kiss*) Have you got anything to say to me?

JACK   Any chance of a cup of tea?

CLAIRE   That's not very romantic. When we're married I'm not going to be a wife who's always at your beck and call.

JACK   Who said anything about marriage?

CLAIRE   At my age, you can't afford the luxury of waiting for some indecisive man to pop the question.

JACK   We've only been seeing each other a couple of weeks. I don't think we should rush into anything.

CLAIRE   I suppose you're right. It's my birthday next month, that would be a good time to spring a little surprise on me.

JACK   I'm not sure I'm ready to settle down yet.

CLAIRE   If you don't soon get a move on you'll be too old to do anything.

JACK   But I'm quite happy with my life as it is.

CLAIRE   Of course you're not, that's the trouble with men, they don't know what they want. I'll make the tea. (*Claire exits to kitchen. The doorbell rings. Jack exits to hall*)

JACK   (*Off*) Hello. (*Annabel enters from hall carrying records. Jack follows her*)

ANNABEL My mum's sent a few sixties classics round for Roy.

JACK I'm sorry but I haven't got a clue what you're on about?

ANNABEL I can't remember his real name, in fact it was all a bit embarrassing. He'd replied to my advert in the lonely hearts column.

JACK Good grief, so you're the twenty-seven year old he tried to pull.

ANNABEL When I first saw him I thought there must be some mistake.

JACK Yes there was a mistake all right.

ANNABEL Anyway, I was telling my mum all about him, and when I mentioned he was the spitting image of Roy Orbison she broke out into one of her hot flushes.

JACK Why would she do that?

ANNABEL She's crazy about Roy Orbison, she can't get enough of him.

JACK So what's that got to do with my friend?

ANNABEL My mum's dying to meet him, she insisted I brought these records round for him to listen to. (*Handing records to Jack*)

JACK Well actually he's a bit tied up at the moment.

ANNABEL She made me promise to arrange a date for her. (*Annabel walks around the room, picking up the family photos and studying them. Jack moves her away from them*)

JACK I'm not sure that's the best of ideas.

ANNABEL She'll be heartbroken if I don't arrange something. Your friend won't be disappointed. (*Looking serious*) She's very good for her age.

JACK	It's just that he's fully booked. He's not able to fit in any more females, at the present time. (*Handing records to Annabel*)
ANNABEL	(*Handing over photo*) She's sent her photo round. It was taken at her keep fit class. She's put her address on the back.
JACK	Very nice indeed. (*Jack puts photo in his pocket*)
ANNABEL	She doesn't want to be tied down with a heavy relationship. She's just looking for a good time.
JACK	Sounds like my sort of woman.
ANNABEL	Most of these records are Roy's greatest hits. Mum's never loaned them out before.
JACK	I'm sure my friend will be very flattered. Leave your mum's number and I'll get him to ring her.
ANNABEL	I've already left her number, but he hasn't rung. (*Starting to cry*) Since my dad cleared off, life's not been easy. At first I said I'd never forgive him, but after a while I thought, well, he is my dad.
JACK	(*Handing Annabel a handkerchief*) Who knows, one day they may get back together again.
ANNABEL	I don't think so. You see dad's got this very special lady friend. Her photos are all over his flat. In any case, Mum doesn't want him back, she's got her bingo and the big 'O'.
JACK	(*Looking vague*) The big 'O'.
ANNABEL	(*Stops crying and blows her nose. Gives the handkerchief back to Jack*) Roy Orbison, he's kept her going through troubled times, that's why your friend could help. Please ask him.
JACK	(*Looking at handkerchief with disgust. He puts it back into his pocket*) Oh all right, I'll have a quick word, just hang on here a minute. (*Annabel hands over the records*)

ANNABEL Thank you. (*Annabel kisses Jack*) Could I use the bathroom, my mascara's running everywhere.

JACK Yes, the bathroom's upstairs, first right.

ANNABEL I won't be a minute. (*Annabel exits to hall. Jack looks through records, then puts them on sideboard and walks to kitchen exit. The doorbell rings*)

JACK Oh no, what now? (*Exits to hall*)

EMILY (*Off*) Hello, could I have a word with Clive please?

JACK (*Off*) It's not very convenient at the moment. (*Emily runs into room followed by Jack*)

EMILY I've got to see him, it's absolutely imperative that I talk to him.

JACK Hang on a minute. (*Looking worried*) Please tell me your name's not Emily.

EMILY It is, how did you know? (*Pause*) Let me guess, you must be Jack.

JACK What on earth are you doing here?

EMILY How much has Clive told you?

JACK Well, let's just say, I wouldn't be happy wired up to a lie detector, with a spotlight on my face.

EMILY He's very lucky, having a friend like you.

JACK I wish I could say the same about him. You've certainly turned his world upside down.

EMILY I'm so sorry, but I just love him to bits. (*With sincerity*) He's the most precious thing in my life.

JACK This is getting worse by the second.

EMILY He phoned to say he was telling his wife about us. I just wanted to make sure I wasn't forcing him into an impossible situation. (*Starting to cry*) You see, I just want him to be happy.

JACK	(*Putting his arms around Emily and handing over the same handkerchief*) Please don't upset yourself. You've certainly brought the sparkle back into his life.
EMILY	Have I? That makes me feel so much better. (*Crying*) I don't want anyone getting hurt. What do you think I should do?
JACK	Go up to the bedroom. (Emily looks confused) I think it's the only free room in the house at the moment. I'll send him up to you.
EMILY	(*Stops crying. Blows her nose, and hands handkerchief back to Jack*) Thank you so much. (*Emily kisses Jack*)
JACK	I suppose being his agent has got some perks. (*Pause*) It's up the stairs … Oh, you probably know the way.
EMILY	Have you ever fallen hopelessly in love?
JACK	No, and I'm going to the doctor tomorrow to get vaccinated against it. (*Pause*) If you bump into any other members of his fan club, just ignore them. (*Emily exits to hall. Jack throws the handkerchief into the waste paper bin. Claire enters from kitchen*)
CLAIRE	The tea won't be a minute.
JACK	I've changed my mind, I'm having a double scotch. (*Pouring out drink*)
CLAIRE	You've started the celebrations a bit early. They haven't even announced the results yet.
JACK	I think I've earned it, care to join me?
CLAIRE	Oh, all right, why not? (*Jack hands Claire a drink*)
JACK	Cheers.
CLAIRE	Cheers. (*Anita, Tracy, Clive and Henry, carrying camera and tripod, enter from kitchen*)
HENRY	I shouldn't be telling you this, but I'm fairly certain you're going to win this competition.

ANITA What, you mean I could soon be on the Caribbean cruise?

HENRY The two other couples have major problems.

JACK (*Aside*) We can make that a hat trick. (*Jack goes over to Clive and whispers in his ear*)

HENRY The husband of one couple didn't inform us that he'd spent ten years of his marriage residing at Her Majesty's pleasure, and the wife of the other couple has got a female friend, who turns out to be more than just a friend.

CLIVE Good grief. I don't believe it.

HENRY Yes, I thought that would shock you. It's reassuring to be in the company of a stable relationship.

CLIVE I'm just popping upstairs.

ANITA (*Shouting*) Not now. (*Quietly*) I mean, don't be long, dearest, we've got to meet the judges. (*Clive runs through hall exit*)

CLAIRE It looks as though your husband's going to have a fiftieth birthday he'll never forget.

HENRY We've got to go through the democratic process of interviewing the other couples. But off the record, start packing your suitcase, you're on your way.

CLAIRE Will you be taking many photos of the happy couple during the cruise?

HENRY No, once we've handed over the tickets, they're on their own. We've decided to give them complete privacy.

ANITA (*Looking thoughtful*) So nobody'll be aware of what's happening?

HENRY Exactly. After all it is a second honeymoon. And who are we to intrude on such an intimate affair?

TRACY You'll have a lovely time, Mum. (*Tracy hugs Anita*)

HENRY	I'll just pop these things in the car, and then we must get going. (*Henry picks up camera and tripod and exits to hall*)
CLAIRE	It looks like it's good news all round.
TRACY	I'm really pleased things have worked out for you and Dad.

(*Clive enters from hall, holding Emily's hand*)

CLIVE	I've got something to tell everyone.
JACK	(*Spitting his drink everywhere*) I really don't think this is the best time.
ANITA	What's going on?
CLIVE	Our marriage is over. I'm in love with Emily.
ANITA	What? Ah … (*Anita faints. Annabel enters from hall*)
ANNABEL	Has anybody here seen Roy?
HENRY	(*Entering from hall*) Everybody ready?

Scene II

As the curtain rises, Anita is sitting on a chair, crying loudly. Claire and Tracy are standing either side of her, each holding a box of tissues. She clicks her fingers, and beckons to whichever one of them she wants a tissue from. There are several plates of savouries on the table and some balloons around the room.

ANITA	I'm going to kill him. Then he'll realise that nobody, but nobody messes with me.
CLAIRE	After all those years of marriage, you must be devastated.
ANITA	I am. Why ever didn't the idiot stop for one more day, then at least I could have won my Caribbean cruise?

TRACY That photographer was off like a shot. I'm surprised he didn't ask what was going on.

ANITA Perhaps someone could tell me what that woman's got to offer that I haven't?

CLAIRE You're depressed enough without comparing yourself to the woman who's got everything. (*Pause*) I'd love to know her secret.

ANITA It's no secret. She latches onto some gullible middle-aged married man, and then takes him for every penny he's got.

CLAIRE Actually, I was talking about her good looks and youthful vitality. She doesn't look a day over thirty. (*Anita cries uncontrollably, she demands tissues from Tracy and Claire*)

TRACY There, there, don't upset yourself, Mum.

ANITA I've given your dad the best years of my life.

CLAIRE It's a pity he didn't leave while you'd still got something left to offer.

ANITA (*Crying*) Isn't it time you were getting home?

CLAIRE No, I'll be supporting you all the way through the divorce.

TRACY Who said anything about divorce? Dad only left yesterday.

CLAIRE We've got to face facts, once they've tasted caviar, they don't want to come back to a bit of old cod. (*Anita cries loudly*)

TRACY (*Getting cross*) Please try and think what you're saying, Claire.

CLAIRE I only meant I can't see him coming back after trading your mum in for a newer model.

TRACY I'm sure Dad'll come to his senses and face up to his obligations.

ANITA You make it sound like a prison sentence.

TRACY Have you informed everyone the party's off?

ANITA Yes, and I've never been so humiliated in all my life. It wouldn't have been so bad if he'd have been run over by a bus or taken hostage in some bank raid.

CLAIRE Whatever did the mayor say?

ANITA Actually, I've told him a little white lie. I said the caterers had let us down.

CLAIRE So what are you going to do with ten dozen vol-au-vents, two hundred sausage rolls and seventy six trifles?

TRACY We could always get the cubs round and have a sponsored binge.

CLAIRE I suppose you won't be needing all those chicken drumsticks now. If they're going spare, I could use a few.

(*Anita cries and demands yet more tissues*)

TRACY (*Handing over tissue*) Oh, Mum, I'm so sorry, are you going to be all right?

ANITA I haven't got much choice, have I?

TRACY It's only when someone's gone, you realise how much you miss them.

ANITA How true that is. (*Pause*) Your dad was the only one who could work the DVD player. Whatever am I going to do now?

TRACY I never thought he'd do anything like this.

CLAIRE He's a man, they can't help it.

ANITA (*Stops crying*) What are you on about?

CLAIRE They've got a one track mind. Sex is the only thing that motivates a man.

TRACY I'm sure Dad's not like that.

CLAIRE Don't you believe it, they say the average male has an erotic thought every three minutes.

ANITA That's the last time I'm having the vicar round for afternoon tea.

CLAIRE It's a pity you didn't spot the telltale signs. You could have nipped it in the bud.

TRACY However can you tell when someone's cheating?

CLAIRE The dust disappears off the aftershave. Mouthwash suddenly appears in the bathroom cabinet. A quicker than normal turnover in the pant and sock drawer.

ANITA (*With great despair*) This is all my fault, I've only got myself to blame.

TRACY Oh, Mum, it's not your fault, you've been a perfect wife.

ANITA I should have spotted that he's been too happy recently. (*Looking thoughtful*) That explains why he was singing in the bathroom yesterday.

CLAIRE You can never trust a man, even when you think their battery's flat, they still seem to produce a spark.

(*The telephone rings. Tracy answers it*)

TRACY Hello … Oh hello, darling, no he hasn't come back … Yes, I'll tell her … All right, I'll be home soon … Love you lots, bye. (Replaces receiver)

CLAIRE (*To Tracy*) Ironic, isn't it? You've sorted out your marriage, and now your mum's is on the rocks. (*Anita starts to cry again*)

ANITA I'm very pleased for you, Tracy.

TRACY Tom sends his regards. He said if there's anything he can do, let him know.

ANITA Would he shoot my husband for me?

CLAIRE	So has your Tom decided to go back to work?
TRACY	(*With elation*) Yes, he's taken another job in the city, in high finance.
ANITA	(*Stops crying*) He's going to be collecting the money in a multi-storey car park.
TRACY	(*Defensively*) Well, it's a start, and who knows where it could lead.

(*The doorbell rings*)

ANITA	(*To Tracy*) Whoever it is, get rid of them. (*Tracy exits to hall*)
TRACY	(*Off*) Hello, Jack, come in. (*Tracy and Jack enter*)
JACK	Hello all, any news?
ANITA	I was expecting you to come up with some answers.
JACK	(*Unconvincingly*) I don't know anything. I'm just as shocked as you are.
CLAIRE	You two are as thick as thieves. You're probably in collusion with him.
JACK	That's not fair. I'm as innocent as a newborn baby.
CLAIRE	That's a laugh. I'm very sceptical when it comes to men.
ANITA	Surely he must have told you something?
JACK	I've hardly seen him for the past month. (*Reassuringly*) I'm sure he'll return with a very simple explanation.
CLAIRE	What, like how he ran off and left his poor defenceless wife in the lurch? I'd like to hear it.
JACK	There's always two sides to every story.
ANITA	Oh that's very rich. Next you'll be telling me that I'm to blame. (*Anita starts crying again*)

CLAIRE	Now look what you've gone and done.
JACK	All I'm saying is, for every wayward man there's a willing woman waiting.
CLAIRE	When we've settled down together, you'll be kept on a tight collar and chain.
JACK	Anybody would think I was a dog.
TRACY	I still can't believe he's done it.
JACK	Nor can I, a forty-two year old, good looking woman with a trim body. (*Aside*) He's certainly hit the jackpot.
CLAIRE	You're not condoning his actions are you?
JACK	(*With envy*) Certainly not. Why should he be allowed to get away with it?
CLAIRE	You two are as bad as each other.
TRACY	We mustn't keep onto Jack, he's told you he doesn't know anything and I wouldn't mind betting that's the truth.
JACK	I've never been a betting man myself. (*Looking awkward*) But it's nice to know that someone's on my side.
TRACY	I'm sure if we could get Dad back home we'd soon sort things out.
ANITA	(*Stops crying*) That could be a little difficult.
TRACY	I can't see why.
ANITA	He'd have a job to put his side of the story with a broken jaw.
TRACY	It's no good dwelling in the past, we should be trying to resolve the situation.
JACK	Your Tracy's talking a lot of sense. Find the reason he left and we're half way to getting him back.

ANITA (*Sarcastically*) Perhaps his new girl friend and I could compare scores? I'd win on the roast potatoes, but she comes out on top in bed.

(*Clive enters from hall*)

TRACY Oh, Dad, whatever have you been doing?

ANITA Well look who it is, Casanova's come back.

CLAIRE (*Walks over to Clive and gives him a look of disgust*) You've certainly put the cat amongst the pigeons.

CLIVE (*Walking over to Anita*) I think we need to talk.

ANITA Let me guess, that tart's sent you back under guarantee?

CLIVE No, it's not like that at all.

ANITA So what's happened, did she try out your fishing tackle and realise you weren't such a good catch?

CLIVE (In a calm voice) Could we discuss this in private, like responsible adults?

ANITA Oh, so it's time to be responsible adults now, is it? You've just been fondling some frustrated female and now I'm supposed to act like nothing's happened.

JACK (*Shaking Clive's hand*) Happy Birthday, mate.

ANITA (*Getting cross*) Oh yes, of course, it's your birthday. Well, after all the treats you've been getting, what I've got will seem rather dull.

TRACY Happy Birthday, Dad. I'll give you your present a bit later.

CLIVE Thank you, dear. (*Clive gives Tracy a kiss*)

ANITA (*Walking over to the balloons*) Now what little surprises have we got for you?

CLIVE I really don't think this is the best time for birthday celebrations.

ANITA	Don't be silly. (*Standing by a deflated balloon*) Here we are, just look at your lovely balloons. (*Anita holds up the deflated balloon*) Oh dear, this one's gone all floppy. Still, you'd know all about that, wouldn't you? (*Walking over to the food*) Now we've got lots of lovely food here.
CLIVE	Actually, I'm not very hungry at the moment.
ANITA	Don't be silly, we've got to eat all this up. We were expecting sixty guests but they haven't arrived. I wonder why? (*Anita gets a small trifle*) Look what I've got here, you just love trifle, don't you? (*Anita pulls Clive's trousers out and pours the trifle into them*) I'm so sorry, I forgot the cream.
CLIVE	I don't want any cream. (*Anita squirts cream into trousers*) Thank you.
ANITA	Now for the big surprise. I've got you a (*Anita lifts a large box from sideboard*) very expensive stereo, and some sixties CD's. (*Anita throws box onto the floor*) Whoops, how clumsy of me. (*Anita kicks the box*)
CLIVE	I want to come back home and live with you.
ANITA	What!! So after the tart's taken you for a test drive and found out you're an M.O.T. failure, you expect me to have you back?
TRACY	I think you should let Dad have his say.
JACK	(*Walking to hall exit*) We'll leave you alone to sort things out.
CLAIRE	(*Sitting on chair*) I'm not going anywhere, I mean, we should be here. That's what friends are for.
TRACY	If I were you Dad I'd pop some more trousers on.
ANITA	I'm afraid that won't be possible. You see I decided your clothes were looking a bit drab. So I've brightened them up. (*Anita opens the sideboard and gets out a pair of trousers that have been cut to bits. She hands them to Clive*) Here's one I did earlier.

TRACY — Oh, Mum, you haven't, have you?

ANITA — Needlework never was my strong subject. I must admit, I even surprised myself how useless I was.

CLIVE — Have I got any clothes left?

ANITA — Two handkerchiefs and a tie. (*Looking pleased*) The rest were write-offs.

JACK — So have you come back to stay?

ANITA — Don't be silly, he's not staying here. (*To Clive*) My solicitor says I can make things almost impossible for you. (*Anita sits on a chair*)

TRACY — Oh, Dad, whatever possessed you to go off like that?

CLAIRE — Tell us everything and don't worry, I'm not easily shocked.

CLIVE — (*Bowing his head*) After twenty-eight years of being faithful, I met a girl and something happened that's difficult to put into words.

ANITA — Is your vocabulary that limited? You had an adulterous affair with some tart.

CLIVE — It wasn't that simple.

ANITA — All right, so she played hard to get before she lit your sparkler.

CLIVE — You're making it all sound so sordid, and it wasn't.

TRACY — Didn't you think of the consequences, Dad?

CLIVE — Yes of course I did, and that's why we spent all last night talking.

ANITA — If you believe that, you'll believe anything.

JACK — I don't think we should be too judgemental, after all, none of us are perfect.

CLAIRE You speak for yourself.

CLIVE We realised that too many people were getting hurt. So she's leaving her flat today and moving up north. (*With great sorrow*) I'll never see her again.

ANITA What a load of drivel. (*Sarcastically*) The truth is you couldn't satisfy the tart, so she's off to find a real man.

CLIVE For the last three hours I've been walking round trying to sort my life out.

TRACY Oh, Dad, you poor thing. (*The phone rings*) I'll get it.

ANITA It's probably that slut, ringing to ask for a refund.

TRACY (*Picking up receiver*) Hello … Yes … WHAT? … So you'll be here in a minute? … Bye. (*Replaces receiver*)

ANITA (*Getting cross*) I don't believe it, she's got a nerve, hasn't she?

TRACY Congratulations. (*Getting excited*) You two have just won the perfect marriage competition.

CLIVE WHAT? }

ANITA WHAT? } Is that supposed to be a joke?

TRACY That was the photographer on his mobile. He'll be here any minute to get pictures of the happy couple receiving their tickets (*shouting*) for the Caribbean cruise.

CLAIRE You've done it! Congratulations.

JACK Well done, I'm so very pleased for you both.

ANITA If anybody thinks I'm going on a cruise with him, they're mistaken.

JACK Let's take one step at a time. There's no need to mention your present predicament.

ANITA So what do we say? Thanks for the tickets, oh and by the way, would you forward the divorce papers on to us?

CLAIRE	If you remember, he said, when you're on the cruise, there won't be any publicity.
TRACY	That's right, once they've handed over the tickets, you're on your own.
CLIVE	Let's go for it. What have we got to lose?
TRACY	Come upstairs, Mum, you'll need a bit of sprucing up. You've just won the holiday of a lifetime.
CLIVE	What about me? (*Pointing down below*) Things are getting a bit gooey.
TRACY	You'll be all right, Dad, just smile and think of England.

(*Claire, Tracy and Anita exit to hall*)

JACK	All right, I've heard the official version, now what really happened? I suppose you got blown out.
CLIVE	No, I've told the truth. After twenty-eight years of marriage, when it actually came to leaving, I couldn't do it.
JACK	So what are you saying, you've bottled out?
CLIVE	My marriage isn't perfect. But my wife's never been unfaithful and I'm too old to become a deceitful husband.
JACK	You've left it a bit late to let your conscience out for the day, haven't you?
CLIVE	I can't be responsible for the break-up of a marriage and lots of people getting hurt.
JACK	But you told me Emily was the girl of your dreams, she was everything you'd ever wanted.
CLIVE	(*With great sorrow*) If only fate hadn't been so cruel, and we'd have met and married years ago. I'd have been living in heaven now.
JACK	You could always take her on as your mistress.

CLIVE	I couldn't cope with the lies and deceit. (*Looking at his watch*) She left two hours ago. We couldn't risk seeing each other again.
JACK	So you've no idea where she's gone?
CLIVE	She's heading up north somewhere. We've agreed never to contact each other again.
JACK	Well, at least you've had a taste of true happiness. That's more than a lot of married men get.
CLIVE	My world's been turned upside down. But now I'm going to make my marriage work.
JACK	After a few weeks everything'll be back to normal.
CLIVE	(*Completely over the top*) Life can never be normal. I daren't even whisper Emily's name for fear someone will spot the telltale signs of a broken heart. Those fleeting precious moments we shared will live in my innermost thoughts until the grave.
JACK	Moving onto more important things. (*Jack examines Clive's neck*) No love bite. You owe me a hundred quid.
CLIVE	What?
JACK	Only joking, we'll call this one a draw.

(*The doorbell rings. Clive exits to hall*)

CLIVE	(*Off*) Come in. (*Clive enters followed by Henry, who is carrying a camera and tripod*)
HENRY	Has your wife recovered from the shock?
CLIVE	(*Looking worried*) What shock?
HENRY	Yesterday, when she found out you could be the winners, she passed out.
CLIVE	Oh yes, of course, I'd forgotten. So much has happened since then.

HENRY	I feel awful that I didn't assist, but I'm very squeamish when it comes to medical matters.
JACK	I gave her the kiss of life, she soon came round.
HENRY	(*Looking at the food*) What a lovely spread, what time does the party start?
CLIVE	(*Looking awkward*) I'm not sure. I mean, my wife's sorting things out, it's a surprise you see.
HENRY	I'm feeling really Hank Marvin.
CLIVE	Hank Marvin?
HENRY	Starving, I haven't had a bite all day. Those sausage rolls look delicious.
CLIVE	Please help yourself, I'm sure we'll have more than enough to go round.
HENRY	(*Helping himself to lots of food*) Thank you very much. (*Anita, Claire and Tracy enter from hall*) Ah, here's your lovely wife. I hope you're fully recovered.
ANITA	(*Looking vague*) Oh yes, I'm much better now, thank you.
HENRY	We interviewed the other couples, but they've got mega problems. In fact, they'd both been totally dishonest.
JACK	You can't trust anybody nowadays.
HENRY	How have you remained faithful, loving and so devoted over all these years?
ANITA	I'm not sure how to answer that.
HENRY	Modest as well. You're certainly a couple of worthy winners.
CLAIRE	Who's going to be making the presentation?
HENRY	I'm afraid that's down to me. The Bishop was doing the honours but got called away unexpectedly.

TRACY	I suppose they're always kept busy with christenings, weddings and funerals.
HENRY	Actually, he's in court today, facing a drunk and disorderly charge.
JACK	Let's hope he's got a convincing prayer lined up for the magistrate.
HENRY	Right, I suggest we get started. (*Handing over tickets and a certificate to Clive*) Congratulations to you both on a long and happy marriage and may the future be even better. (*Henry shakes Clive's hand and kisses Anita*) Now, if you'd hold the tickets and certificate in view of the camera, I'll take a couple of photos. (*Anita stands away from Clive, who is holding tickets and certificate*) Closer please, show the world how blissfully happy you are. (*Anita moves nearer Clive. Henry takes a photo*) One more, expressing your true feelings.
JACK	This should be interesting. (*Henry takes another photo*)
HENRY	That's it, folks, and may I say you're an example to the rest of us.
CLAIRE	When will you be putting this in the paper?
HENRY	Next Tuesday. By that time, you'll be on your cruise. We're using the headline "What's their secret?"
JACK	That sounds very appropriate.
HENRY	I must be off. I won't be bothering you again, and have lots of fun on your second honeymoon. (*Henry grabs a handful of food and stuffs it in his mouth*) This food really is delicious. (*Henry picks up camera and tripod*) Goodbye, and the best of luck.
JACK	(*Aside*) They're going to need it. (*Henry exits to hall*)
ANITA	(*Grabbing the tickets from Clive's hand*) You won't need these, I'll be finding someone else to take.
CLIVE	But I thought we were going to try and work things out?

ANITA	Well, you thought wrong then.
TRACY	Oh, Mum, please don't be too hasty, give Dad a chance.
ANITA	I am giving him a chance. (*Pause*) To find a good solicitor while I'm away.

(*Doorbell rings*)

JACK	That's probably the photographer come back for some more food.
TRACY	I'm telling him the truth. (*Exits to hall*)
ANITA	Don't you dare say a word.
TRACY	(*Off*) Hello
ANNABEL	(*Off*) I need to come in, it's very urgent. (*Annabel and Tracy enter*)
TRACY	It's not very convenient at the moment. (*Annabel walks over to the wedding photos and looks at them carefully*)
ANNABEL	I knew I'd recognised the face.
JACK	Oh no, they say it never rains but it pours.
ANNABEL	(*Walking towards Clive - she goes past him to Anita*) You know my dad don't you? You've been having an affair with him for the past five years.
ANITA	(*Trying to look innocent*) I don't know what you're on about.
CLAIRE	(*Looking confused*) I can't keep up with all this, it's doing my head in.
ANNABEL	Perhaps this'll help refresh your fading memory. (*Getting a photo from her pocket and handing it to Anita*) I took it from my dad's flat earlier today.
ANITA	(*Sitting down on sofa*) Oh dear, so you're Don's daughter?

CLIVE	(*Looking totally confused*) Would someone tell me what's going on?
ANNABEL	My dad left five years ago for another woman. (*Annabel snatches photo from Anita and hands it to Clive*) Recognise her?
CLIVE	(*Looking at photo*) You mean to tell me, for the last five years you've been having an affair? (*Clive sinks into chair*)
TRACY	Oh, Mum, how could you?
ANNABEL	When Dad realised I'd found out who you were he asked me to deliver this. (*Annabel hands a piece of paper to Anita, she reads it*)
CLAIRE	I'm losing track of what's happening. Could we slow down please?
ANNABEL	I've been wanting to meet the woman who broke up my family.
JACK	I just can't believe I'm hearing all this.
CLIVE	But what about our marriage?
ANITA	(*Looking up*) That was over years ago, we've only stuck together through habit.
CLIVE	So you're saying you don't want to carry on?
ANITA	Carry on with what, the sham we've been living? The children are independent, we've got totally different outlooks on life, there's nothing holding us together now.
CLIVE	So all this sanctimonious stuff about me breaking up the marriage was just an excuse?
ANITA	I must admit things seemed to be going my way.
CLIVE	And there's no prizes for guessing who you'd be taking on the cruise.
TRACY	Mum, I just can't believe you'd do that.

ANITA   I didn't want to hurt your dad's feelings, but I've been looking for a way out.

CLIVE   So that's it then. Twenty-eight years of marriage down the pan.

ANITA   I'm sure we'll reach an amicable arrangement. Especially now you've met a new friend.

CLIVE   (*Getting cross*) If you'd have been listening, I told you she's already left, so that I could save my marriage. What a joke.

TRACY   (*With sympathy*) I'm so sorry, Dad. I don't know what to say.

CLIVE   I still can't believe you've been unfaithful for five years.

ANITA   The very fact you hadn't noticed says everything about our relationship.

CLIVE   That explains why you came home knackered after the WI had that talk on the mating habits of a rabbit. You'd been putting the theory into practice.

ANITA   I'm sorry. But, on the other hand, I'm pleased it's all out in the open.

ANNABEL   Dad's moving to Australia, isn't he?

ANITA   Yes, and he's asked me to go with him.

CLAIRE   Australia, but that's over the other side of the world.

ANITA   His firm's asked him to set up a new office. He'll be looking for a secretary. (*To Claire*) You've got all the necessary qualifications.

JACK   (*Aside - with elation*) They say that every cloud's got a silver lining.

CLAIRE   I can't leave my Jack, we've got plans, haven't we, dearest?

JACK   I couldn't possibly stand in the way of your career.

ANITA (*Walking to hall exit*) Come on Claire, let's at least go and have a talk. I've been wanting you to meet Don for ages.

TRACY (*Getting cross*) You're not just walking out like that, are you?

ANITA It's probably best if I give your dad time to think. Oh, by the way (*handing tickets to Clive*) I won't be needing these tickets, I'll be too busy sorting out other matters.

CLAIRE (*Giving Jack a hug*) See you later, Jack.

JACK (*Unconvincingly*) I can't wait.

(*Anita and Claire exit to hall*)

TRACY Oh, Dad, this is absolutely awful. What are you going to do?

JACK Don't worry about your dad, I'll be looking after him. You get off home to your husband.

ANNABEL I must go. I'd better tell Mum what's happening. If only I could find out where Roy's gone.

JACK Tell her she could be in for a surprise tonight. Roy's thinking of calling round.

ANNABEL (*With exuberance*) Oh, that's wonderful, I'll go and let her know.

TRACY Are you sure you'll be all right, Dad? (*Giving Clive a hug*) Give me a ring if you need anything. I'll call in tomorrow and see how you are. (*Annabel and Tracy exit to hall*)

CLIVE Is this a nightmare, or have I just lost my wife and the girl of my dreams in the space of a day?

JACK Well, let's put it like this. You won't be waking up.

CLIVE Five weeks ago I was just your average married man. The most exciting event of the week was pouring the gravy over my Sunday roast. (*With sorrow*) I won't even have that to look forward to now.

JACK All right, so tomorrow we'll get you a cookery book, then you can make your own.

CLIVE My whole world's falling apart.

JACK (*Pulling a photo from his pocket*) There's always another ace in the pack. The Roy Orbison outfit's in my car. (*Jack hands over the photo*) You've got a real winner here. She's ready, willing and by the look of her, she's certainly able.

CLIVE Not tonight, I don't really feel in the mood. (*Hands photo back to Jack*)

JACK In that case, we'll head to the pub and get down to some serious drinking.

CLIVE Would you think me rude if I said I need to be alone for a while to sort my life out?

JACK Not at all. (*Looking at photo*) Would you think me rude if I said I'd like to be Roy Orbison for the night? This lady looks a bit tasty.

CLIVE Go ahead, enjoy yourself. I'll see you tomorrow.

JACK How about a hundred quid if I get a love bite?

CLIVE No chance, get out of here.

JACK You take care. Enjoy the rest of your birthday, and remember, tomorrow's another day.

(*Jack exits to hall. Clive picks up goldfish bowl and holds it in the air*)

CLIVE It's just you and me against the world now, Suzie.

(*Clive plays a record of Paul McCartney singing "Yesterday." He sits on the sofa, staring into space. After a few seconds the doorbell rings. Clive turns record low then exits to hall*)

EMILY (*Off*) May I come in for a minute?

CLIVE (*Off*) Emily.

(*Clive and Emily enter*)

EMILY   I just had to come back.

CLIVE   Oh Emily, I'm so very pleased, but we'd agreed never to see each other again.

EMILY   No, you don't understand, last night when you took me out to dinner I left my handbag in your car. It's got everything in it, including my car keys. I can't leave till I've got them.

CLIVE   You're not going anywhere. I'll never let you out of my sight again. (*Clive picks up the competition tickets, and holding them in the air*) I'm taking you on honeymoon. We're going on a Caribbean cruise.

EMILY   I beg your pardon?

CLIVE   I'll explain everything later.

EMILY   Happy Birthday darling! (*Clive and Emily go into a passionate kiss*)

Blackout

BY THE SAME AUTHOR

LOVE BEGINS AT FIFTY (Modern Farce)
M3 F6
This fast and furious farce was first published in 1998 and has never looked back as production follows production. Described by one critic as being up to the highest standard of Ray Cooney - praise indeed.

IT MUST BE LOVE (Farcical Comedy)
M3 F6
Another hilarious play by Raymond Hopkins, with a wedding as the main topic. Enjoyed a highly successful summer season at Torquay.

LOVE AND MONEY (Farcical Comedy)
M4 F4
Another farce from one of the masters of the art. "Never a dull moment – easily staged in one set"   AMATEUR STAGE

LOVE AND PERFECT HARMONY (A Comedy with Music)
M4 F5
This is the fifth play by Raymond Hopkins. Here we have the trials and tribulations of the local choral society. Can be performed with a minimum of scenery.

OTHER PLAYS PUBLISHED BY SILVERMOON PUBLISHING
www.silvermoonpublishing.co.uk

Nativity
by Jonathan Hall
(2m, 3f)
It's December 1979 and class 2G are getting ready for the school Nativity. Gemma wants to be Mary but because she's got a big loud voice she's the narrator, and anyway Sarah her best friend is far loads prettier than her, everyone says so. And as for Kirsty- she doesn't even get a look in, not that she cares, she's bothered about showing her knickers in the practical area. And of course there can only be one choice for Joseph, and that'd have to be Tony, everyone's favourite, complete with his thirteen colour biro. And Nicholas? In love with Sarah and dreams of flying through the milky way with her in the TARDIS? He's always going to be the Innkeeper.

Nativity is about the play we've all been in. About tea towels on heads and coconut-shell donkey hooves. Dinner ladies and toilet roll angels, reading books and Blue Peter. It's about our six year old selves, the adults that shaped us, the dreams that lit our days- and the people we have become.

I Gave You My Heart
by David Muncaster
(2f)
Kate has received a parcel through the post from her ex-boyfriend. Her sister, Jenny thinks it is sweet, sending her a nice little parting gift. But Dan isn't sweet according to Kate. He's a freak a weirdo. And whatever is in that box is somehow related to the last thing that he wrote on Kate's Facebook page – "I gave you my heart"

Flushed
by Ron Nicol
(3f)
It's a singles night, and Jan and Meg are taking a break in the Ladies Room. Jan is criticising Tara, unaware that Tara is hiding in one of the toilet cubicles. When Tara's
presence is revealed a fight ensues and Jan confesses the reason for her jealousy. Then Meg discovers that the door to the room seems to be locked, and the succeeding series of mishaps and misfortunes ruins Jan's appearance and assurance. Tara eventually manages to open the door, but on the threshold of escape they find that Meg is trapped in one of the cubicles.

A Beginner's Guide To Murdering Your Husband
by David Muncaster
(3f,2m)
This play is presented as though it is an instructional video that the audience are watching being filmed. Maddy will present a variety of methods for disposing of an unwanted husband, aided by Jim, her real life husband, and her faithful employees. But is she really trying to get rid of her husband? Is the video just a ruse to lull him into a false sense of security? The parallels with their real life relationship give Jim plenty to worry about but, as the play reaches its its climax, we realise that nothing is what it seems. Criss-cross indeed!

Understanding Women
by Devon Williamson
(3f,1m)
Mike, Dave and Julian spend a weekend in a garden shed determined to break an age-old mystery. Armed with a case of beer, a box of girlie magazines and a holy book they are going to "understand women". What they discover is not quite what they expected. Understanding Women is a comedy play for both sexes!

Crazy Ladies
by Devon Wiliamson
(5f,1m)
Pamela Browne has organized a 25 year reunion for her four best High school friends. From the moment Kay, now a chocoholic gun toting funeral director, arrives the wheels begin falling off Pamela's meticulously planned weekend. Added to the mix is Sandy, who is now a Nun, Dianne, married the school nerd and a mother of eight sons, Rachel, a runaway teenager on a mission to dig up some dirt on her mother, and Shaun, the greasy motel janitor. This outrageous comedy is a rollercoaster ride of emotion.

The only monthly magazine **passionate** about amateur theatre

subscribe online:
www.asmagazine.co.uk

Scan the QR Code to join us on Facebook

Follow us on twitter @amateurstage

www.ingramcontent.com/pod-product-compliance
Lightning Source LLC
Chambersburg PA
CBHW061500040426
42450CB00008B/1437